All the Right Moves

ACM Distinguished Dissertations

1982

Abstraction Mechanisms and Language Design
by Paul N. Hilfinger

Formal Specification of Interactive Graphics Programming Language
by William R. Mallgren

Algorithmic Program Debugging
by Ehud Y. Shapiro

1983

The Measurement of Visual Motion
by Ellen Catherine Hildreth

Systhesis of Digital Designs from Recursion Equations
by Steven D. Johnson

1984

Analytic Methods in the Analysis and Design of Number-Theoretic Algorithms
by Eric Bach

Model-Based Image Matching Using Location
by Henry S. Baird

A Geometric Investigation of Reach
by James U. Korein

1985

Two Issues in Public-Key Cryptography
by Ben-Zion Chor

The Connection Machine
by W. Daniel Hillis

1986

All the Right Moves: A VLSI Architecture for Chess
by Carl Ebeling

The Design and Evaluation of a High Performance Smalltalk System
by David Michael Ungar

All the Right Moves

A VLSI Architecture for Chess

Carl Ebeling

The MIT Press
Cambridge, Massachusetts
London, England

PUBLISHER'S NOTE
This format is intended to reduce the cost of
publishing certain works in book form and
to shorten the gap between editorial preparation and final publication. Detailed editing
and composition have been avoided by
photographing the text of this book directly
from the author's prepared copy.

Library of Congress Cataloging-in-Publication Data

Ebeling, Carl.
  All the right moves.

  Originally presented as the author's thesis
(Ph. D.—Carnegie-Mellon University, 1986).
  Bibliography: p.
  1. Chess—Computer programs.
2. Computer architecture. 3. Integrated
circuits—Very large scale integration.
I. Title.
GV1449.E24   1987   794.1'7   87-3178
ISBN 0-262-05035-8

*To my parents
Donald and Lisette*

Contents

List of Figures

List of Tables

Preface

The question of whether machines can exhibit intelligence on a par with human intelligence has long been an intriguing one. Chess is often used as a benchmark for machine intelligence, partly because chess skill exemplifies many of the facets of human intelligence such as perception, judgement and calculation, and partly because it is a contest that pits man directly against machine. The advent of electronic computers with the ability to calculate far faster than anything before possible sparked interest in programming a machine to play chess. As early as 1950, Shannon laid the foundation for the basic algorithms for computer chess. Right from the start, then, chess provided the new field of Artificial Intelligence with a suitable arena for research.

There had been sufficient progress in computer chess by the mid-1960's to encourage some researchers in Artificial Intelligence to predict that a computer would beat the world champion within a decade. Yet in spite of all the recent progress in technology and in the field of Artificial Intelligence, computer chess performance at the Master level has remained elusive. This is partially due to underestimating the tremendous amount of knowledge and judgement that a chess Master uses to evaluate which lines of play to pursue, and partially due to the difficulty of applying this knowledge in a computer program.

This thesis describes a new architecture used by the Hitech chess machine to achieve a new plateau in computer chess performance. This architecture uses fine-grained parallelism to perform the complex computations required by move generation and position evaluation extremely quickly. This enables Hitech to search very quickly and knowledgeably, a combination that yields very high performance. Since its debut in 1985, Hitech has played over 50 rated games, achieving a USCF rating of 2352, some 150 points higher than other computers and near the top of the Master class.

Although this research may appear to have implications only within the area of computer chess, we believe that the architecture described in this thesis is applicable to other problems. Computers are able to compute extremely fast, but this does not translate into intelligent behavior because we do not yet know how to encode complex knowledge and apply it effectively. We believe that a viable solution to many problems is to combine an extremely fast search, which takes advantage of the computer's strength, with the application of as much knowledge as we know how to apply. This thesis describes an architecture for applying knowledge in an efficient manner so that the speed of the search is not compromised.

We begin by introducing the problem of computer chess and giving some background on the algorithms that have been developed. We then describe the new architecture used by Hitech for generating moves and evaluating positions and discuss how VLSI (Very Large Scale Integration) can be used to implement these functions efficiently. The remainder of the Hitech chess hardware is then presented and the actual operation of the chess machine is described. We then analyze the performance of this architecture in the context of Hitech and discuss some of the lessons learned in building an actual machine. The last chapter summarizes the results of the thesis and discusses some of the implications for other problem areas.

Acknowledgements

I thank my committee, Bob Sproull, Hans Berliner, Raj Reddy and Ken Thompson for the care with which they read this thesis and for the many helpful comments they made. I am grateful to my advisor Bob Sproull whose counsel I could always trust and whose experience and knowledge were a valuable resource. I especially thank Hans Berliner, with whom I have spent many fruitful hours discussing the ideas in this thesis. It was he who first interested me in this topic and he who kept the momentum going when my energy flagged. Hans also supplied the majority of the chess knowledge in Hitech's evaluation function. My good friend Ed Frank offered ideas, argument, and encouragement. Much of what I know about building hardware I learned from Ed.

A project of this magnitude is possible only with the help of many people. Andrew Palay was the first to recognize the effect that VLSI technology could have on chess move generation. Many of the ideas in this thesis were developed with his collaboration. The reliability of the Hitech hardware is due in large part to the care and dedication of Larry Slomer. Without his help and companionship, building Hitech would have been much more difficult. Gordon Goetsch wrote much of the host software, integrating the chess analysis routines written by Hans Berliner with the hardware driver routines and the user interface. Murray Campbell played an important role in helping design the host software, suggesting ideas and finding bugs through hours of testing. H.T. Kung stepped in at a crucial point to provide the host hardware we needed and the Archons project kindly lent us hardware resources and advice when we were just starting. The move generator chips were fabricated by DARPA through the MOSIS fabrication service which has provided excellent support to the University VLSI research community.

Finally I thank my wife Lynne who has shared the experience of graduate school. Her encouragement and confidence got me through the difficult times when the task seemed impossible.

1

Introduction

There are two schools of thought as to the best way for computers to play chess. The first approach examines only a few alternative lines of play and attempts to understand the resulting positions by applying a large amount of chess knowledge and experience to reason about the effects of every available course of action. This reflects the way humans play chess and has a certain amount of aesthetic appeal. The second, so-called brute-force approach, searches a much larger part of the game tree to discover the effects of each course of action, applying only a small amount of chess knowledge to each position. This takes advantage of the primary strength of computers: extremely fast computation.

There are disadvantages to both methods and it is difficult to argue which is the right or most natural way to solve the problem. There is no reason to believe that the best way for a computer to play chess is to mimic the reasoning of a human being. On the other hand, until now the ability of humans to play chess has been far superior to that of computers. The deep understanding approach has failed largely because of the extremely difficult task of encoding all relevant chess knowledge and bringing it to bear on the problem. Programs that have tried this can play reasonable chess most of the time, but invariably falter because they have not reasoned through all the implications of all the lines of play. The brute-force approach plays excellent tactical chess because it can see all outcomes that can take place within several moves, but fails to understand the importance of the long-range strategic aspects of the game since it cannot take the time to perform more than a cursory evaluation of the positions it examines.

Much indirect experimentation has been done to determine the correct balance between speed and knowledge, but over the past decade computer chess has become the province of the fast brute-force searching programs, primarily because we understand better how to use computers for fast, simple computation than for complex knowledge-based understanding. Yet it is the opinion of many chess experts that searching speed alone is not sufficient to produce top quality chess play—for computers to penetrate the top levels of human play, they must both search fast and know a lot.

This thesis presents a parallel architecture for move generation and position evaluation that greatly reduces the effect of the traditional tradeoff between search speed and knowledge. This architecture applies fine-grained parallelism to these two subproblems, allowing these complex operations that usually limit the speed of the search to be done extremely quickly. The speed of the move generator is independent of the number of legal moves in a position, and the speed of the evaluation depends only logarithmically on the amount of knowledge encoded in the evaluation. That is, doubling the knowledge base adds only constant time, the time required for a single addition, to the time required to perform the evaluation. In practice, this means that the amount of analysis performed by the evaluation does not slow the search.

Although the amount of hardware required to implement the architecture for these two problems is large in terms of the number of gates required, the architecture is eminently suited to VLSI since communication requirements both on and off-chip are limited. This thesis describes a VLSI implementation for both move generation and position evaluation that demonstrates the effectiveness of this architecture on these problems. The VLSI move generator was designed and fabricated, and has been incorporated into a chess machine called Hitech. The move generator searches about 200,000 positions per second and includes all the ancillary circuitry necessary for it to interface cleanly with the rest of the system. A hardware simulation of the VLSI position evaluator is also included in Hitech, allowing its capabilities to be measured as well.

Hitech has achieved the highest level of play ever attained in computer chess. From its debut in May, 1985, through March, 1986, Hitech played in 51 rated tournament games, achieving a rating of 2352, 150 points higher than the previous best. This places Hitech in the top 1% of all rated U.S. players. Figure 1.1 places Hitech's performance in the context of previous efforts in computer chess. The previous jumps in performance that occurred in 1966 and 1976 resulted from increasing the speed of the search, either by optimizing the search or by using special purpose machines or supercomputers. The increase in performance achieved by Hitech results from the combination

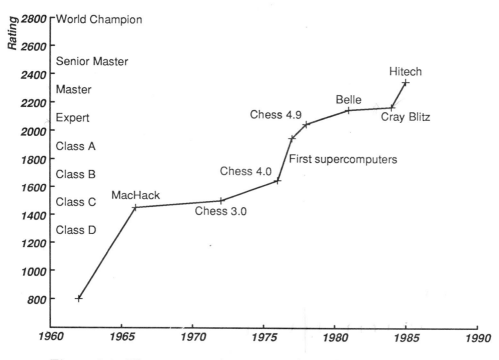

Figure 1.1: *The progress of computer chess-playing programs.*

of speed and knowledge made possible by the architecture presented in this thesis.

The approach of applying fine-grained parallelism to searching avoids the problems inherent in applying a coarser parallelism that either splits the search among many processors or pipelines the search process. The first suffers from the communication overhead that is required to make the individual searches aware of each others' work in order to avoid unnecessary computation. Research into making such an approach work in practice has not been successful in finding ways to utilize more than a few processors[18,10]. Pipelining the search suffers because the path through the search tree cannot be predicted since it depends on the values computed dynamically at each node. Such data dependency always causes problems in pipelined systems.

1.1   Computer Chess Programs

The principles of computer chess have not changed much since Shannon elaborated them 35 years ago[26]. The problem is to choose the correct move from the given position, that is, the move that results in the best chance of winning. This is done by hypothesizing each legal move in turn and determining its consequences by evaluating the resulting position. The best move is the one that results in the best position. This analysis is much too primitive since it does not consider the opponent's possible responses. The answer is to determine the opponent's best response to each of the player's moves by applying the same procedure, except that the opponent's best move is the one which results in the *worst* position for the first player. Extending this even further gives rise to a recursive minimax search that examines the tree formed by examining all moves and responses starting from the root position.

This search consists of three components: search control, move generation and position evaluation, which operate in the sequence shown in Figure 1.2. The search control executes a simple depth-first tree traversal, invoking the move generator when extending a branch and the position evaluator when it has reached a leaf node. The minimax procedure is done by assigning values to each interior node based on the maximum or minimum value of its sons. As the search moves from one position to the next in the search tree, the board state on which the move generator and position evaluation operate is changed by the update and backdate operations.

Although there have been many refinements to the basic minimax search, such as the α-β algorithm, it remains central to all chess playing programs. In particular, none of these refinements, which will be described in the next chapter, introduce computational requirements anywhere near as great as that of the move generator and position evaluator. From Figure 1.2, the search procedure appears very simple. Exactly how complicated are each of these operations?

1.1.1   Update/Backdate

The update and backdate operations are invoked when the search moves between adjacent points in the search space to change the state on which the move generator and position evaluator operate. A simple representation of this state is just the location of all the pieces on the board. The difference

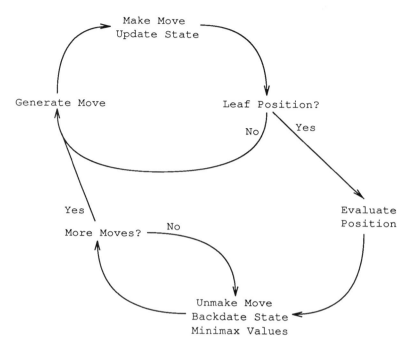

Figure 1.2: *The sequence of operations executed when searching the game tree.*

between neighboring positions is the result of making or unmaking a single move, which affects only two squares except in the relatively rare cases of castling and *en passant* moves. This means that the state can be updated incrementally by changing only the two squares affected by the move. This can be done by two or three primitive state updates depending on whether or not the move is a capture. One update is required to remove the captured piece, if any, from the destination square, another to remove the moving piece from the origin square, and another to place it on the destination square. We call each of these incremental changes *halfmoves*. The backdate procedure performed when unmaking moves reverses each halfmove in turn. Thus the update and backdate operations that change the state as the search moves from position to position are very fast, requiring about the same amount of time as traversing the tree and minimaxing values.

1.1.2   Move Generation

The move generator is generally the component that sets an upper bound
on the speed of the search. Far more complicated than the tree traversal
operations, the move generator must compute the legal moves of each piece
according to the rules of chess. Moreover, as we shall see in the next chapter,
the order in which the move generator produces the moves is crucial to the
efficiency of the search. Thus the move generator must not only generate
the moves but order them as well, so that the best moves are considered
first. The next chapter enumerates some of the alternative methods of move
generation and describes some of the attempts to speed this operation with
special-purpose hardware. Chapter 3 describes our solution to this problem.

1.1.3   Position Evaluation

Unlike move generation, which has a well-defined task, position evaluation is
open-ended. There is essentially no limit to the amount of analysis that can
be applied to each position examined by the search. Programs are subject
to a tradeoff between the search speed and the amount of knowledge to be
applied to evaluation. Some programs like TECH[12] have opted for speed
and reduced the evaluation function to the bare minimum, counting only
the material balance. This simple evaluation is very inexpensive to compute
since the material count can be maintained incrementally in much the same
way as the position state is maintained. This results in a tactically wise but
positionally ignorant program. Other programs have applied a great amount
of knowledge to the evaluation at the expense of slowing the search. The trick
is to find just the right balance between speed and knowledge. Chapter 4
describes a way to do evaluation that effectively decouples these issues. This
evaluation hardware reduces the time for evaluation to about the same as
that required by the search control, dramatically increasing the amount of
knowledge that can be applied to understanding each position.

1.1.4   Features Common to Move Generation and Position Evaluation

The difference between move generation and position evaluation is less than
it appears. Both operate on a state in the problem space to produce a set of
legal moves in one case and a value in the other. While the end results are

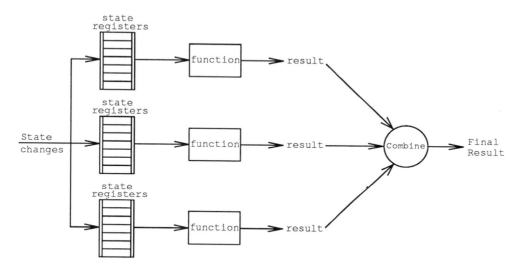

Figure 1.3: *An overview of the proposed parallel architecture for move generation and position evaluation.*

different, each bases its calculations on the relationships between the pieces on the board. The move generator looks for relationships that imply legal moves, while position evaluation looks for relationships that imply strong or weak positions based on factors such as pawn structure, king safety, and piece placement.

The parallel architecture that we propose for these problems is outlined in Figure 1.3. The problem of generating legal moves or evaluating a position is divided into many independent components, each of which is computed in parallel by the functional units shown in this figure. Each component is computed by a simple function over some subset of the board state. This state is maintained within each functional unit to avoid the problem of communicating information from a set of centralized state registers to a large number of units. This means that state is duplicated where it is used by more than one unit. For example, each unit that needs information about a particular fact, such as the white queen being on e3, has a register for that fact. These registers are updated whenever a halfmove that affects this information is broadcast.

The results produced by the individual functional units are combined differently by the move generator and the position evaluator. The individual results in the move generator are boolean values indicating whether particular moves are legal. These are combined via a selection algorithm that chooses the estimated best move. In position evaluation, the results are values which are merely summed to produce a final value. In either case, the combining operation is one that can be performed in O(log) time in the number of individual results. This can be realized in practice using a priority encoder tree for move generation and an adder tree for position evaluation.

A real difference between the two is that the legal move computation can be fixed since the rules of chess allow only a fixed number of moves that can ever be possible. The move generator needs to look only at this fixed set of possible moves for legal moves. Conversely, there is no *a priori* limit to the number of factors that position evaluation may need to consider. Our design of the position evaluation generalizes the design used for move generation to allow the evaluation hardware to be programmed. This not only allows the evaluation to be tuned and expanded as its deficiencies are discovered, but enables the program to modify the evaluation function during the course of the game.

This latter idea allows the evaluation hardware to be used much more efficiently. Instead of having to implement an evaluation function that can understand any position occurring during the beginning, middle, or end of the game, the program can tailor the evaluation function to compute those factors known to be important in each particular phase of the game. This is done by examining the material on the board, the location of the kings, and perhaps even the arrangement of the pawns to decide which factors are important and which can be ignored. This substantially reduces the amount of hardware required to perform the evaluation.

1.2   The Structure of the Thesis

Background material and related work will be presented first in Chapter 2. This will describe the advances that have been made in computer chess since Shannon's first paper and describe other efforts that have used special-purpose hardware to speed the search. This chapter provides the background necessary to understand the material presented in the remainder of this thesis.

Chapter 3 presents our parallel architecture as a solution to the move generator problem and describes the design of a VLSI move generator chip, 64 of which are used in Hitech's move generator.

Chapter 4 analyzes the requirements of position evaluation and describes how a more general form of the architecture used for move generation can be used for evaluation. A VLSI chip for position evaluation is described along with how it is used to perform some of the more complicated evaluation computations.

Chapter 5 describes the structure of the Hitech chess machine and the remaining components that are used together with the move generator described in Chapter 3 and the evaluation function described in Chapter 4.

Chapter 6 measures the performance of Hitech in general and the move generator and evaluation hardware in particular. This leads to conclusions about how well this hardware supports searching and how the implementation might be optimized to produce better performance.

Chapter 7 summarizes the contributions of the thesis and suggests topics for further research.

2

Background

The principles of computer chess have long been established, starting with the paper by Shannon in 1950[26] that outlined a program consisting of three parts: the minimax search algorithm, a legal move generator used by the search to move from one position to the next, and a position evaluator that estimates the end result of a line of play by analyzing the terminal position in the line. Developments over the last three decades have seen refinements to these three components but no major change to the overall structure of the program. The minimax search examines all possible lines of play from the position in question to determine the one that produces the best result. While it is theoretically possible to examine all lines until a win, loss or draw has been established, in practical terms the search can pursue only a few moves for each side before halting and evaluating that particular line of play. In chess, where there are an average of 35 legal moves in each position, an eight ply minimax search (four moves ahead for each side) must visit 35^8 or about 10^{12} positions, far beyond the capability of any current computer. In fact, in spite of laying the foundation for further chess programs, Shannon scoffed at the idea of programs doing complete searches since they could only look a very few moves ahead.

A major improvement to the minimax search algorithm was discovered independently by several researchers in the late 50's and first described by Newell, Shaw and Simon[21]. This improvement, called the α-β procedure, greatly reduces the size of the search tree that the minimax algorithm must examine. This is done by using information established during the course of the search to prove that certain moves cannot affect the outcome and therefore can be ignored by the search. In particular, the search of the first subtree of a position establishes a lower bound, called α, on the value of the position. Any subsequent move by the opponent that can serve only to lower this value can be ignored. A complete exposition of the α-β search algorithm can be found in the article by Knuth and Moore[16]. In the best of situations the α-β search can search about twice as deeply as the equivalent minimax search. This reduces the observed, or *effective*, branching factor to the square root of the real branching factor. In chess, this means that the α-β search examines an average of about 6 moves in each position instead of 35. This best of situations occurs when the moves from each position are examined in an optimal order, which is very important when considering the design of the move generator.

Some further optimizations can be applied to the α-β search. If a good estimate can be made of the eventual result of the search, then the bounds can be set before the search begins with some additional savings. This type of narrow-window search[11] performs α-β cutoffs before the actual bounds on the search value have been established. If the estimated bounds are not accurate, then the search must be performed again to find the real value. This can be taken a step further by assuming that the first move is the best move and searching the remaining moves with a zero window[11]. If the first move is best, then all the remaining moves result in a low cutoff. If not, the better move will result in a high cutoff indicating that the move is better but not establishing any value. If only one move is better, the exact value is irrelevant; if more than one move is better, these moves must be again searched to determine which is better.

Other developments over the years have included refinements to the position evaluation component. Shannon originally suggested several simple measures for evaluating a leaf position. The most important of these was material advantage, but piece mobility and pawn structure were also included. One aspect of evaluating the leaf nodes that quickly became apparent was that the position may not be a quiet one; that is, it may change drastically after the next move if, for example, there is a piece *en prise* or perhaps the king in check. Even threats of check or capture make a position active and thus susceptible to evaluation error. This problem is countered by doing a *quiescence search*[11] to establish the true value of a leaf position after the active aspects have been allowed to play themselves out. Although there are differences of opinion as to what constitutes a quiet position, the most often used criteria include allowing outstanding captures and responses to check before performing the evaluation.

While the move generator and search are fairly stable components of a chess program, the position evaluation usually evolves continually as more chess knowledge is incorporated. While chess programs play tremendous tactical games, their understanding of long range positional strategy is still quite poor. Most programs attempt to overcome this by evaluating the leaves more thoroughly with respect to positional aspects of the game such as king safety and pawn structure. The other area where searching fails is in the endgame where simple deductive reasoning can formulate winning plans much more effectively than blind searching. There has been substantial effort trying to incorporate positional and endgame factors into the position evaluation with only moderate success, and chess programs often find themselves using their tactical skills trying to save lost positions.

A different approach to the problems of brute-force search is the use of a more selective search which chooses only the most promising lines of play for investigation. This was called a type B strategy by Shannon[26] and in its simplest form relies on a plausible move generator. Other approaches have relied on shallow searches or some high level analysis of the position to reduce the branching factor[4,23]. These efforts have been less than successful since there are sometimes obscure lines that must be played to win or avoid loss. Experience with selective search has not proved successful against the standard complete α-β search.

Two very important contributions to search efficiency have been the ideas of iterative deepening[28] and the hash table[31]. The hash table is especially effective when used along with iterative deepening. Iterative deepening is a search strategy that first performs a shallow search followed by ever deeper searches until the desired depth is reached or time is exhausted. This means that the search for the best move at each game position actually comprises a set of *search iterations*. We will refer to the search iteration that searches to ply n as the nth search iteration. Iterative deepening allows time to be used efficiently by not permitting deep searches that cannot possibly finish before the allotted time expires. The time taken by each successive iteration is used to estimate how long the next iteration will take and a reasonable decision can be made whether or not to continue.

The hash table is used to cache the values established by the search at the interior nodes of the search tree. Since the tree is actually a graph— the moves made to reach a position can be made in different orders—the value saved in the hash table allows the search to avoid performing an identical search when a position is reached a second time. When used together with iterative deepening, the hash table can also improve the order in which moves are examined. This is done by saving the move that establishes the value of a position along with the value in the hash table. Since this move is the best move to the depth searched by the previous iteration, it is more reliable than the best move as estimated by the move generator. As will be shown in the next section, this alone is sufficient to result in near-optimal α-β performance.

The results of other computation done during the course of the search can also be cached to reduce the amount of recomputation required. This is usually done for complex components of the evaluation function[2]. For example, the detailed evaluation of pawn structure can be a very time-consuming computation which need not be performed repeatedly on positions with the same pawn structure. The use of another hash table based only on the pawns can be used to save the results of previous evaluations. The effect of this optimization has been described in detail with respect to the Cray Blitz program[20].

Another optimization that has gained wide use is the idea of killer tables[13]. There are many positions encountered in a search that are similar in that there is one move that serves as a refutation, known as a *killer* move. A refutation is a response to a move which demonstrates that that move does not work; that is, that it is worse than some other move that has already been tried. This can happen in two ways, giving rise to depth-based and response-based killer tables. Depth-based killers occur in positions in which many of the moves have the same refutation. Since the position resulting from each move is different, the refutation found while examining the first move is not available from the hash table when searching the second. A depth-based killer table is used to save the refutations found for other moves at the same depth. With response-based killers, a move which is legal in many different positions in the search tree almost always has the same refutation. Again, since the positions all vary slightly, the hash table can offer no refutation. With this type of table, the refutations are saved according the move being refuted. Killer-tables are most effective when the killer move is not an obvious move, but one that takes some effort for the search to find.

2.1   Move Ordering and Search Efficiency

The order in which moves are considered is crucial to the efficiency of the search. As first shown by Slagle and Dixon[27], when moves are examined in

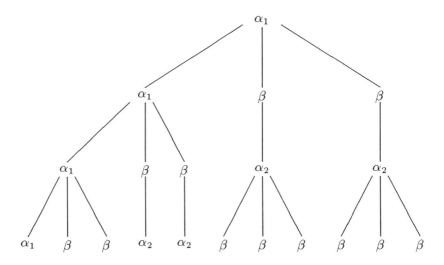

Figure 2.1: *An optimal α-β tree of degree 3.*

the best order, the α-β search algorithm can reduce the effective branching factor to the square root of the real branching factor, allowing the search to go twice as deep. More precisely, the number of leaf positions considered is

$$bf^{(d+1)/2} + bf^{d/2} - 1. \tag{2.1}$$

The question is how efficient the search can be in practice. An examination of how the α-β search performs in the optimal case gives insight into how move ordering should be done to increase the efficiency of the α-β search. Although intuition suggests that all moves must be tried in the best order to achieve the optimal efficiency, this is much too strong a condition. In fact, for almost half the positions in the tree the actual move ordering is irrelevant, and for most others only one good move is required.

The tree in Figure 2.1 shows an optimal α-β tree of degree 3. Informally, at odd depths all moves must be examined since the search is trying to find the best move for the first player. At even depths, the search is looking for a response by the second player that refutes the first player's move. Along the principal variation, the situation is reversed since the first move cannot be refuted and all responses by the second player must be examined to find the best response. The nodes in this tree fall into three classes:

1. The root and all first successors of α_1 nodes are α_1 nodes. All the successors of α_1 nodes must be searched to establish which is best. If the tree is optimal, the best successor is searched first. If the tree is not optimal, then the number of α_1 successors is equal to the number of times a successor returns a value greater than the maximum of those already examined. We call this number A, and if the moves are ordered randomly, $A = H_n$ where H_n is the nth harmonic number.

2. All but the initial successors of α_1 nodes and all successors of α_2 nodes are β nodes. For β nodes, only the single successor that establishes a refutation needs to be searched. If the tree is not optimal, then more than one successor may be examined before a refutation is found. The number of moves searched from a β node we call B.

3. All successors of β nodes are α_2 nodes. All the successors of α_2 nodes must be examined to complete the proof that the parent is a refutation, but since the result does not affect the result of the search or the α-β bounds, the order in which the successors are examined is irrelevant.

This analysis reveals that a sufficient, but not necessary, condition on the move ordering to obtain the optimal search tree is that the one best move from each position be tried first; the remainder can be ordered arbitrarily. The reason that this ordering condition is too strong is that the ordering is irrelevant at α_2 nodes and that there are several valid refutations at many β nodes. This explains the great effect that the hash table has on search efficiency. The hash table saves the best move found for each position in the nth search iteration. If these moves continue to be best during the $n + 1^{st}$ search iteration, then the hash table provides the optimal move ordering except at those positions at depth $n + 1$, which were not examined during the nth search iteration.

While it is difficult to analyze α-β trees precisely when an optimal ordering does not hold, we can estimate the number of terminal nodes visited by a search in terms of the measures A and B. The number of terminal nodes in the tree rooted at an α_1 node is:

$$C_{\alpha_1}^n = AC_{\alpha_1}^{n-1} + (bf - A)C_{\beta}^{n-1} \qquad (2.2)$$

where n is the depth of the tree and bf is the branching factor. Here we assume that the branching factor and the values of A and B are uniform over the entire search. The number of terminal nodes in the tree rooted at a β node is:

$$C_\beta^n = BC_{\alpha_2}^{n-1} \tag{2.3}$$

and the number of terminal nodes in the tree rooted at a α_2 node is:

$$C_{\alpha_2}^n = bf\, C_\beta^{n-1} \tag{2.4}$$

When $A = B = 1$, the equations reduce to:

$$C_{\alpha_1}^n = C_{\alpha_1}^{n-1} + (bf - 1)C_\beta^{n-1} \tag{2.5}$$

and

$$C_\beta^n = bf\, C_\beta^{n-2} \tag{2.6}$$

Table 2.1 shows how the size of the search depends on the values of A and B. We have chosen an 8 ply search with an average branching factor of 35 as a typical case. The results are given as a ratio with respect to the optimal case where $A = B = 1$. The effect of using a hash table to improve the move ordering is to decrease the average value of A and B near the root of the tree. Table 2.2 shows how the search size is reduced if the values of A and B are reduced to 1.2 for nodes within 6 ply of the root. The search sizes actually observed in Hitech are about 1.5 times the optimal.

Several observations based on this analysis affect the design of the move generator.

- From Table 2.1 and Table 2.2 it can be seen that the value of B has a greater effect on the search efficiency than the value of A. This is because A affects only the size of the search of the first move while B affects the size of the entire tree.

- Generating the best move at α_1 nodes is very difficult: if it were not so, then selective search based on a deep analysis of the α_1 nodes would be a viable alternative to a complete search. The move generator usually can do no better than produce reasonable moves first, that is, moves that do not have obvious refutations. If we assume that of the bf successors of an α_1 node only 20% on average are reasonable, then trying reasonable moves first reduces the value of A from H_{BF} to $H_{BF/5}$. Since $H_{35} = 4.15$ and $H_7 = 2.59$ the move generator does not have a great effect on the value of A. Fortunately, the search efficiency is not as sensitive to the value of A as it is to the value of B.

Table 2.1: *The effect of A and B on the size of an 8 ply search. The search size is given as a ratio with respect to the optimal case where A = B = 1.*

A	B							
	1.0	1.2	1.4	1.6	1.8	2.0	2.2	2.4
1.0	1.00	1.77	2.89	4.44	6.50	9.17	12.55	16.74
1.5	1.48	2.56	4.09	6.16	8.88	12.36	16.70	22.04
2.0	2.09	3.51	5.50	8.15	11.58	15.92	21.28	27.80
2.5	2.87	4.71	7.21	10.52	14.74	20.02	26.48	34.28
3.0	3.91	6.23	9.35	13.40	18.52	24.84	32.52	41.71
3.5	5.28	8.19	12.04	16.96	23.10	30.61	39.65	50.38
4.0	7.10	10.73	15.44	21.38	28.70	37.57	48.14	60.60
4.5	9.52	14.02	19.76	26.89	35.58	46.00	58.32	72.72
5.0	12.73	18.28	25.24	33.77	44.05	56.25	70.55	87.14

Table 2.2: *The effect of the hash table on the search size can be seen when the values of A and B of nodes within 6 ply of the root are set to 1.2.*

A	B							
	1.0	1.2	1.4	1.6	1.8	2.0	2.2	2.4
1.0	1.00	1.19	1.39	1.58	1.78	1.97	2.17	2.36
1.5	1.11	1.32	1.53	1.74	1.95	2.16	2.37	2.58
2.0	1.22	1.45	1.67	1.90	2.12	2.35	2.57	2.80
2.5	1.35	1.59	1.83	2.07	2.31	2.54	2.78	3.02
3.0	1.49	1.74	1.99	2.24	2.49	2.75	3.00	3.25
3.5	1.63	1.90	2.16	2.43	2.69	2.96	3.22	3.49
4.0	1.79	2.07	2.34	2.62	2.90	3.17	3.45	3.73
4.5	1.96	2.24	2.53	2.82	3.11	3.40	3.68	3.97
5.0	2.13	2.43	2.73	3.03	3.33	3.63	3.93	4.22

- The majority of moves from α_1 and α_2 nodes are blunders, leaving a piece *en prise*. Such moves are easily refuted by some 'obvious' capture. Moreover, knowing the absolute best move from a β node is not necessary since a blunder can usually be refuted by any of several moves.

We refer to this as the *refutation principle* and it relaxes somewhat the requirements of the move generator. In fact, the move generator can reduce the average value of B to close to 1 if it can identify these refuting captures. Since the search efficiency is very sensitive to B, the effort applied to finding these refutations is rewarded by a much faster search.

- The value of B depends on the value of A. If the best move at α_1 nodes is not examined first, then the responses to subsequent moves are more difficult to refute. This effect is minimized if reasonable moves are tried first since a reasonable move will result in a value that is almost as good as the value of the best move.

- Statistically, the values of A and B near the root have the same effect on the *average* search efficiency as their values near the leaves. However, a change in A or B at one node near the root has a much greater effect on the search time than a similar change at one node near the leaves since the size of the affected subtree is much larger. Moreover, changes in A and B near the root are usually caused by changes in the value of the search from one iteration to the next, possibly indicating that the previous best move is now a losing move or that there is a better move to be made. It is just these situations for which the search must be efficient enough to see the correct move.

- During the $n+1^{st}$ search in iterative deepening, the best move from an α_1 node may well change if there are several reasonable moves. Therefore the average value of A, while decreased by the use of the hash table and iterative deepening, is not likely to be reduced to near 1. On the other hand, the refutations stored at β nodes are very likely to continue to be refutations in the deeper search, and thus the average value of B in most cases is very close to 1. In general, only if the value of the search changes radically from the nth to the $n + 1^{st}$ search will a refutation from the previous iteration be inadequate.

Part of this thesis will address the effect of move ordering, iterative deepening and the hash table on search efficiency and the relationship between these three factors. Understanding this relationship is crucial when making decisions about the tradeoffs that exist when doing move generation and ordering. A move generator with perfect move ordering would make the search unnecessary since the first move would be the correct move. But the only way we know how to order moves well is through a deep search. In fact, one measure of how well moves are ordered is the depth of the search conducted to determine their value. A move generator that uses a two ply search to order moves will result in a more efficient search than one which uses a one ply search, which in turn is better than one which orders moves randomly. In fact, if the move generator orders the moves according to a one ply search, the last ply in the search is unnecessary since it yields the same information about the moves as the move generator. In practice, of course, there is no way to know where the last ply occurs because of quiescence considerations.

Another way to look at the effect of the hash table on move ordering is that the move ordering at interior nodes—at least for the first move—is determined by a search of depth $h - 1$, where h is the distance from the node to the leaf nodes, since that is how deep the previous iteration searched the node. The move generator determines how good the move ordering is for nodes not in the hash table, generally those near the leaves. This views iterative deepening as progressively improving the move ordering at all nodes in the tree, particularly at the root.

2.2 Move Generation

The task of the move generator is to determine the set of legal moves from each position in the search tree. The search process then chooses a move at a time from this set with which to extend the search tree. As shown in the preceding section, if the best move is chosen first in all the important positions, the resulting search attains maximum efficiency. Moreover, for almost half the positions, the β positions, the remaining moves are not used at all. Ideally then, the move generator does not produce all the moves for a position at once, but only the best of the moves remaining to be tried. By doing this the move generator saves the time used to generate moves that are never tried and produces an optimal ordering as well. Move generators that run on sequential processors are hard pressed to generate moves one at a time in any reasonable order and chess programs usually resort to producing and sorting all the moves. In fact, the evaluation function is often used to order the moves based on the value of the position reached by each move. Although the work of move generation can be avoided at β positions if the hash table provides a refutation, this refutation must have been produced by the move generator during some previous iteration.

The standard method of generating moves is very simple: it considers each piece in order and computes the set of squares to which it can move based on its type. A move is legal if the destination square does not contain a friendly piece and, for sliding pieces, if the path to the destination is not blocked. If sliding piece moves are generated starting with the squares next to the moving piece, then remaining moves along a ray can be ignored after a piece blocking the path is discovered. This process will in fact generate illegal moves that result when the king is left in check and should be called a *pseudo-legal* move generator. We will continue to call these moves legal and assume that those that are illegal can be easily filtered out by determining whether the king is in check after the move is made.

Many programs take advantage of the parallel bit processing available on a per word basis on serial machines by using *bit-boards*[11]. These are 64 bit values where each bit represents a fact about one square of the board. Typical bit-boards are used to keep track of friendly pieces, enemy pieces, open squares, friendly knights and so on. All moves to or from a square for a particular piece type can also be represented as a bit-board. This can reduce the problem of generating all moves for one piece to simple boolean operations on bit-boards. For example, all the moves of one knight are generated by the operation:

$$\textbf{knight}_{x_o, y_o} \cdot \neg\textbf{friendly}$$

where **knight** is a table of bit-boards for all legal knight moves, (x_o, y_o) is the location of the knight, and **friendly** is the bit-board of friendly pieces. All the knight captures are generated by the operation:

$$\textbf{knight}_{x_o, y_o} \cdot \textbf{enemy}$$

where **enemy** is the bit-board of all enemy pieces. It helps to have a computer with a wordlength of 64 and machine-level instructions such as priority encode for identifying which bits are set in a word. Using bit-boards for generating sliding moves is more complicated since it is difficult to recognize blocked moves with simple bit operations.

The problem with these methods of move generation is that the moves are made according to a piece moving from an origin square whereas move ordering is more often determined by the value of the captured piece on the destination square. According to the refutation principle, the move to try first is the one that captures the piece left *en prise* by the opponent. One strategy for the move generator would be to attempt to capture the piece just moved by the opponent, but this is expensive since it involves working backwards towards moves that may not exist. Most move generators simply generate all moves and then order them, sacrificing the factor of two in time spent producing all the moves at the β nodes.

Since the change from one board position to the next is small, in most cases affecting only two squares, there would be an advantage to computing moves incrementally. As moves are made or unmade, the set of legal moves would be modified to include moves that become legal and to remove moves that are made illegal. Unfortunately, the computation involved is usually more than would be used to simply generate the moves from scratch. For example, removing a piece from a square can enable many sliding moves that were previously blocked, and placing a piece can block many other sliding moves. Added to these changes are all the changed moves of the moving piece and the deleted moves of the captured piece. The resulting changes may involve over half the set of legal moves. While some of the data structures that are used by a chess program such as bit-boards are computed incrementally, the legal moves themselves are not.

2.2.1   The Ideal Move Generator

Before we describe other hardware move generators that have been proposed, let us describe the characteristics of an ideal move generator based on our observations of the α-β search algorithm. This will give some criteria for judging these move generators. The move generator should be sufficiently fast that it does not limit the speed of the search. It should produce one move at a time, the best of those moves not yet examined. Although this is more than is required by the optimal search, it recognizes that an optimal move ordering is not achievable, so at times more than one move must be generated before the best move is found at α_1 positions or a refutation is found at β positions. The move generator should maintain enough state for each active search position to be able to produce the next move quickly when required by the search. The move generator should produce a minimum of illegal moves that result when the king is left in check. Although these illegal moves can be detected quickly and easily, in some tactical positions where more than half the moves may be illegal, the move generation overhead can become substantial. Finally, the move generator should be able to determine whether any given move is legal in the current position. While this is not a strict requirement of the move generator, this capability allows the hash table to be used for improving the move ordering and for optimizations such as killer tables.

While all of the hardware move generators that have been proposed compute the set of legal moves for an arbitrary position, some do not include all the features that make the move generator a useful part of a chess program.

2.3   Previous Hardware Move Generators

The first significant attempt to build hardware to support move generation was the CHEOPS project at MIT[19]. This hardware, called CHARM, was based on an idea that has become the basis for most hardware move generators that have been built or proposed. The idea is to simulate the moves of the pieces on the board in hardware. An 8 by 8 array of cells, each representing a board square, is connected by wires according to the way pieces move. Some wires communicate queen moves, others communicate knight moves, and so on. Each cell contains a register whose contents indicate the piece occupying that square. Moves are generated by instructing one cell to assert the move wires corresponding to its piece. If the piece is a sliding piece, the signals propagate through neighboring cells until a blocking piece is encountered. The set of moves is determined by which cells are reached by a move signal. The CHARM hardware also includes priority circuitry that allows the program to determine which piece to move next and which destination squares are enabled.

It is difficult to assess how well this hardware performed because of the lack of reports of its use in actual chess programs. It was intended to be used as a hardware accelerator for traditional chess programs, but little provision was made for evaluation. Moreover, it appears that move ordering would have to be done as in traditional software programs since the moves are generated on the basis of origin square; there is, however, some capability for looking for refutation moves by generating signals out from a likely destination square to find pieces that can move there.

Babaoglu refined this move generator idea to include move ordering as part of the move generation procedure[1]. The refutation principle indicates that the best capture should be tried first, which generally means taking the highest valued piece possible. This piece is identified by instructing *all* cells with a friendly piece to assert move signals and noting the squares that come under attack. The highest valued piece, called the *victim*, is identified using a priority encoder. The attacking piece is then identified by sending signals back along the move wires that were asserted to find the victim. The lowest valued piece that can capture the victim is identified using another priority encoder. This move generator was never constructed, although a prototype containing two cells was built and tested. From the description, it appears that all moves are generated at each position since there is no mention of a stack for disabling previously generated moves.

This design was further refined by Thompson and Condon and incorporated into Belle[9], the Bell Labs chess machine that was the first computer to become a Chess Master. Belle's design includes the priority circuitry and context state required to make the move generator truly useful. The move generation and move ordering are performed in essentially the same way as in Babaoglu's design, except that only one move is generated at a time. A disable stack consisting of one bit per square is used to mark which moves have already been generated. These moves are then disabled when generating the remaining moves. The Belle hardware also uses the same wires and priority circuit for the find victim and find aggressor functions, reducing the hardware requirements.

Although Belle's move generator has excellent performance and provides most of the functions that we outlined for the ideal move generator, it has some shortcomings. First, although its move ordering is very good, especially with respect to refutations, it is based on capture information only, which corresponds roughly to a one ply search. If information about the opponent's moves were also available, an approximation of a two ply search could be used to order moves by projecting recaptures. This information can be computed only at great cost by Belle's move generator. Second, using this style of move generation to determine whether one particular move is legal requires generating all the moves to the destination square and testing whether the move in question is produced. Thus detecting illegal moves suggested by the killer table or hash table can incur substantial overhead.

Of greater concern if one contemplates using VLSI to implement this type of move generator is the large amount of communication between the different components. The Belle move generator consists of 64 similar circuits arranged as the squares of a chess board, and there are more than 50 wires between each circuit and its neighbors. In VLSI, the area needed to run this many wires might well consume more area than the active circuit elements.

Moreover, if this move generator is too large to fit on a single chip, the communication required between chips causes a problem both in terms of the number of package pins required and time required to ripple the move signals from one end of the board to the other. On the whole, it does not appear that the Belle move generator lends itself easily to VLSI implementation.

A modified version of this type of move generator was implemented as a VLSI chip at the University of Toronto[25]. The circuit was reduced to a feasible size by time-multiplexing one column of the 8 by 8 array. Since the move signals are propagated in eight different directions, many cycles are required to generate moves. Moreover, the order in which moves are produced is determined by the sequence in which the cycles are executed, and move ordering is performed after all moves have been produced. Generating all the moves does avoid the cost of an on-chip context stack, but requires an average of over 300 machine cycles, taking about 100 microseconds with the stated 3 MHz. clock. This performance is much less than is required for a high performance chess machine, especially since no move ordering is performed.

Another VLSI design of this move generator architecture is currently underway at CMU[15] with an entire Belle-style move generator being integrated on a single chip. This is being done by reducing the size of the circuit, primarily by removing the on-chip context stack and redesigning the priority circuitry, and by using improved technology in the form of a 3 micron CMOS technology. This chip has the potential of reducing the size of a high-performance chess processor to a very few chips, allowing many such processors to be used in parallel. Two problems have yet to be solved: how to include a competent evaluation function and how to make effective use of more than a few processors in a parallel α-β search[10].

2.4   Hardware for Position Evaluation

There are fewer instances of hardware designs for position evaluation than for move generation. There are fast incremental methods for performing position evaluation in software as was done in TECH[12], but none for move generation. In fact, about 90% of the time in TECH was spent performing move generation. Position evaluation is not fixed like move generation. That is, the chess knowledge that should be part of the evaluation is difficult to identify and is subject to change as experience is gained with the program.

It is much more difficult to make hardware evaluation flexible than software evaluation. The only documented special purpose hardware for position evaluation is Belle's evaluation.

2.4.1   Belle's Evaluation

Belle's evaluation function uses both standard incremental evaluation and special hardware for performing complex evaluation[9]. This special hardware evaluates king safety, pawn structure, and board control. The king safety component is done by a simple table lookup based on the position of the king and the presence of pawns in front of the king. The pawn structure evaluation uses a table lookup based on the number of pawns on adjacent files. The board control evaluation is done analogously to the way move generation is performed. A set of 64 cells representing the squares of the board are connected as in Belle's move generator. All moves are generated over a sequence of eight cycles and each square accumulates a figure that represents the control of that square. During each cycle, moves are propagated along one of the eight ray directions, except that moves are not blocked by pieces that can move along the same ray direction.

2.5   A New Approach

The special-purpose hardware solutions that have been used to date for move generation and position evaluation all use the same idea, that of simulating the way pieces move on the board. This is an *ad hoc* approach that closely follows the structure of the problem. Our approach is somewhat different. We have designed an architecture that allows many different functions over the board state to be computed in parallel using fine grained parallelism. Move generation is performed by computing the legality of *all* possible moves and ordering the resulting set of legal moves using heuristics that predict the value of each move. Since the information about all the moves for both sides is available, the moves can be ordered better than when using just the capture heuristic. This results in a more efficient search than obtained by previous move generators. This architecture also works well for position evaluation. The many different components of the evaluation function are computed in parallel and combined in $O(log)$ time using an adder tree.

A crucial feature of this architecture is that it maps well into a VLSI implementation. Unlike other approaches to the problem, this architecture can be implemented using a wide range of chip densities, allowing advanced circuit technology to be used to reduce the chip count and increase the speed of the circuit. The next chapter describes our approach to move generation, presents the VLSI architecture we use, and gives the details of the chip that does move generation for Hitech. The following chapter discusses position evaluation and shows how this architecture can be used to solve that problem as well.

3

The Move Generator Architecture

The speed of the operator that provides the means to move from one point in the search space to the next places an upper bound on the size of the search space that can be examined. In chess this is often the factor that limits the search size since the move generator is rather complicated due to the rules that govern how pieces may move. Chess programs typically balance the time spent generating moves with that spent performing position evaluation, but since our aim is to perform the evaluation almost instantaneously, the speed of the move generator remains the limiting element in the search. In the previous chapter, we analyzed the effect of move ordering on the efficiency of the α-β search algorithm and showed that the optimal efficiency is achieved if the best move is examined first at each node. Moreover, if the first move examined at β nodes provides a refutation, the remaining moves can be ignored. Thus generating all the moves in all positions is a waste of time. Unfortunately, typical software move generators are forced to generate all moves since it is difficult to determine *a priori* which move to generate first. In fact, the position evaluation is often used to order the moves based on shallow searches. This effort can be supported at positions near the root where move ordering has a large overall effect on the size of the subtrees that must be searched, but if the search is to cover a large area, a better alternative is required for generating and ordering moves for the majority of nodes in the tree.

This chapter outlines a fast parallel move generator, describes a general VLSI architecture for its implementation, discusses the solution used for move selection, and ends with a description of the details of the actual implementation.

3.1   A Parallel Circuit for Move Generation

The software and hardware move generators described in the previous chapter are concerned with only the moves of the pieces that are actually on the board in a given position. Software move generators generally compute the entire set of moves in the most convenient order and then sort them according to some set of heuristics or perhaps even with shallow searches depending on the importance of the node in the tree. By contrast, Belle works backward from the most interesting destination square, producing the moves to that square one at a time. The hardware solution that will be described here concerns itself with every move that could *ever* be possible, computing which are actually legal in the current position, and selecting what is considered to be the best move from that set one at a time as required.

We call the set of moves that could ever be possible the *ever-possible* moves, which can be described as the set of triples {piece, origin, destination} in the cross product (Piece × Square × Square) that are allowed by the rules of chess. This set can be enumerated by examining all the moves that could ever be made by each piece in turn. For example, one can place the queen on each of the 64 squares in turn, listing those destination squares to which the queen could move on an empty board. Another way to enumerate this set is to examine each square in turn and list all the moves that can be made to that square by the different pieces. Figure 3.1 shows the ever-possible moves to the square e4. We could extend the definition of an ever-possible move to include the piece, if any, on the destination square, but this would result in increasing the size of the set by a factor of six with little benefit.

An ever-possible move is actually legal in a position if the following three independent conditions are met:

- The *origin* condition: The appropriate piece must be present on the origin square.

- The *destination* condition: The destination square must either be empty or be occupied by an opponent's piece.

- The *sliding* condition: For sliding moves (queen, rook, bishop and two square pawn moves), the squares between the origin and destination square must be empty.

As an example, consider the move bQ/b4–e4. For this move to be legal, the

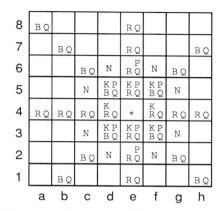

Figure 3.1: *The set of ever-possible moves to the square e4.*

black queen must first be on the square b4, the square e4 must be empty or contain a white piece, and the squares c4 and d4 must be empty.

The computation required to decide whether each of the ever-possible moves is legal is straightforward, requiring only a handful of gates operating on information about the state of the squares affecting the move. A parallel move generator comprised of one of these simple circuits for each ever-possible move can compute the entire set of legal moves very quickly in parallel. A key observation made years ago by Allen Newell is that there are relatively few, about 4000, ever-possible moves for each side. Until recently, building a move generator based on computing the legality of all ever-possible moves has not been feasible. However, VLSI technology has made it possible to build circuits comprising several thousands of gates on a single chip. We shall now investigate the possibility of using this technology to build a move generator based on the idea of computing every ever-possible move.

3.1.1   Computing the Ever-Possible Moves

The simple circuit shown in Figure 3.2 performs the computation for the ever-possible move bQ/b4–e4. The input to this circuit is a subset of the state variables that represent the board position, and the output is a boolean value indicating the legality of the move. The straightforward implementation of the state variables is an 8 by 8 array representing the board, where each array location is a 4-bit value encoding the piece occupying that square of the board. The state variables are easily maintained incrementally: with the

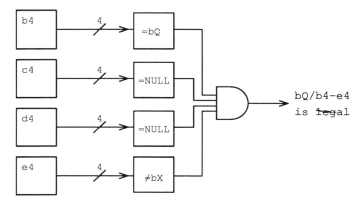

Figure 3.2: *The circuit to compute whether the ever-possible move $bQ/b4$–$e4$ is legal. This represents the average sliding move where there are two squares between the origin and destination squares.*

exception of the relatively rare cases of castling and *en passant*, moves affect only two squares and thus two writes into the array are sufficient to update the state variables when a move is made or backed up.

Each move computation circuit is connected to the state variables that affect that move. In the example shown in Figure 3.2, there are connections to four different squares for a total of 16 wires. For 4000 move computation circuits, this would come to 64,000 wires between the state variable array and the move computation circuits.

This number of wires can be reduced substantially by taking advantage of the redundancy in the computation performed for similar moves. For example, there are 24 moves for the black queen from the b4 square and each of these share the same origin square condition. The gate that recognizes this origin condition can be included with the state variable array and a single signal routed to each of the 24 move computation circuits. Similarly, all the moves to the same square share the same destination condition, which can be computed once, and the single boolean result wired to each move computation circuit. The sliding condition needs only a boolean value for each of the intervening squares indicating whether the square is empty. Sharing this redundant computation reduces the wires input to the average computation circuit from 16 to 4, the total number of wires to 16,000, and each move computation to a single AND gate.

The resulting circuit comprises 256 bits of state in the state variable array, 768 gates (64×12) for the origin conditions, 64 gates for the sliding conditions, 64 gates for the destination conditions and about 4000 gates for the actual move computations. If one were to implement this with standard TTL parts, the circuit would comprise approximately 2000 packages, a large but not overwhelming amount of hardware. Unfortunately, even more hardware is required to perform the move ordering and selection which must take the 4000 boolean outputs of the above circuit and produce a single legal move.

This problem appears to be a good candidate for VLSI implementation where several thousand gates can be implemented on a single chip. The problem with the solution outlined above is the large number of wires required to communicate the values of the state variables to the move computation circuits. If we assume that each of the 16,000 wires is an average of 250λ long with a pitch of 6λ, standard for metal wires, then the total area taken by the wires alone is $24 \times 10^6 \lambda^2$, or equal to a 10mm.$\times$10mm. chip in 4 micron technology. By contrast, the 5000 gates would take only $12.5 \times 10^6 \lambda^2$, assuming each used an area of $50\lambda \times 50\lambda$. Moreover, this calculation of the wiring area assumes that a regular wiring pattern can be devised, something that may not be possible.

An attempt to reduce the wiring could be made by grouping together the computation circuits that share inputs. However, only one of the inputs can be shared among circuits with an improvement of perhaps 20% in the amount of wiring. If one groups the move computations by origin square, then the wire communicating the origin condition can be shared but the wires for the other conditions cannot be shared. The symmetric situation occurs if the computations are grouped by destination condition.

While the preceding analysis is based on broad estimates, it is sufficient to show that a straightforward VLSI implementation is unworkable, even without considering the other tasks required by move generation such as move selection and maintaining state during a depth-first search. A possible solution to this implementation problem would be to partition the circuit onto several chips, thereby reducing the amount of wiring and circuitry on each chip. Unfortunately, the wiring problem is even greater across chip boundaries because of the limited number of package pins, typically on the order of 100 even for large chips. Clearly there needs to be some way of reducing the number of wires that connect the components of the circuit if the circuit is to be implemented with a reasonable number of parts.

The key idea of the move generator architecture that permits a reasonable implementation is that of duplicating the state variables throughout the move computation circuits so that the inputs to those circuits are available where they are used instead of being communicated through many different wires. Of course the state variables themselves must be maintained as moves are made, but this requires far less communication. Only 10 wires are required to communicate the address and data when writing into the state variable array: 6 bits of address for the square location and 4 bits of data to indicate the new contents of the location. While these 10 wires must be routed throughout the circuit to all state variables, this can be done with a regular layout to minimize wiring space. Moreover, while these address and data wires are long and have substantial capacitance, with only 10 wires to drive, the resources in terms of power and drivers can be allocated to reduce the delay associated with driving these wires. In the previous situation where there are many wires, the space and power required to reduce the wiring delay is simply not available.

There are some important points to be made about this circuit transformation. First, it makes a single chip implementation more feasible by drastically reducing the communication between circuit elements on the chip. Second, if the entire circuit is too large to fit on one chip, and this is the case with current technology, the circuit can be partitioned almost arbitrarily onto several chips. This is important since it allows the partitioning to be done to support move selection and also makes it possible to partition the circuit into several identical chips with an associated saving in design and fabrication costs. Finally, it allows the implementation to track advances in technology. While the initial implementation was done using 64 chips, it could easily be reimplemented as 16 or perhaps 8 chips with currently available technology.

One can view the move generator as a write-only memory where the memory output is a set of functions of the memory state. The memory is not the usual one, however. A single write instruction modifies many different memory locations, and since a single memory value is used by many different functions, each location is replicated in each function circuit to minimize the amount of wiring required. The speedup is achieved by the parallelism that occurs as several thousand discrete calculations are performed in parallel on the memory contents.

One can also view move generation as a large pattern recognition problem for which there are 8000 possible features, 4000 moves for each side, to be recognized in a board position. Each of the 8000 circuits acts as a feature recognizer that looks for one particular pattern corresponding to one ever-

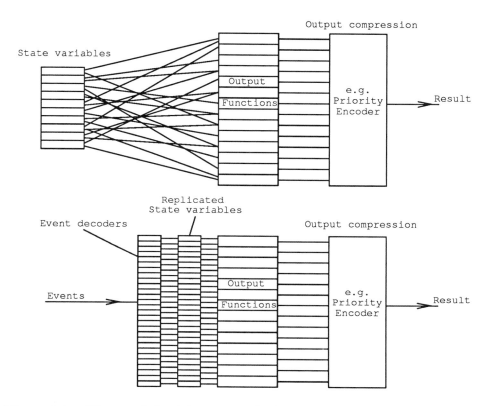

Figure 3.3: *The tangled wiring network that carries the state variables to the function circuits in the first circuit is replaced by a single event bus that communicates the change in the state variables. Copies of the state variables used by each function are kept within the function circuit itself.*

possible move. As the board changes, the information about the change is broadcast to all the recognizers, each of which determines whether a feature is present or absent. The result is the parallel computation of the 8000 move functions with very little communication overhead either in terms of time or chip area.

The move generator as described so far consists of a large number of private state variables that are updated simultaneously using halfmoves, and a large number of move computation circuits that compute either true or false for each ever-possible move. The result is a circuit that computes a new set of legal moves as fast as the board position is changed. The other part of the problem is accessing this set of legal moves. There is no point in computing the set of legal moves instantaneously if it takes 1000 or even 100 probes to retrieve them. This second part of the circuit depends largely on the move ordering algorithm, and will be described in Section 3.1.3. This algorithm chooses one move from the entire set of legal moves in a series of pruning steps that takes only $O(log)$ time in the number of ever-possible moves. A two-level priority encoder reduces the set from 4000 possible moves to 64 in one execution cycle; then a distributed voting sequence further reduces the set to one in at most four cycles. This selection process uses local information to perform sophisticated move ordering on the entire set of legal moves.

3.1.2   Partitioning the Move Generator

If we assume that we can design each move computation circuit in an area of $100\lambda \times 100\lambda$, then the 4000 move computations require $40 \times 10^6 \lambda^2$, larger than any chip that can be made with current technology. Moreover, even simple move selection requires substantial area, and there remains the issue of maintaining the state of the move generator as the tree is searched. All this points to the necessity of partitioning the circuit onto more than one chip.

How the move generator is partitioned depends strongly on the move selection algorithm. The result of the move generator circuit we have just described is a vector of 4000 boolean values. The *true* values in this vector must be extracted and presented as moves. One way to do this is with a multi-level priority encoder that reduces the 4000 inputs to a 12-bit index representing the first legal move. The output value from such an encoder can be used as an address into a table to produce the move in whatever format is most convenient. Implementing a priority encoder of this size is not impossible, and with suitable optimization of the number of levels and circuit parameters, the delay would be acceptable, on the order of 15 to 20 gate delays. The real problem with this solution is that the moves would always be presented in some fixed *a priori* order. Since the description of the ever-possible moves does not include the contents of the destination square, this ordering cannot take into account the effect of captures. This would result in an untenable move ordering. If the ever-possible move description were modified to include the captured piece, then the moves could be arranged statically to include capture information at the expense of a six fold increase in the circuit size. Even this is not sufficient to produce very good move ordering since it does not take into account those cases in which a capture does not work because the captured piece is well guarded.

3.1.3 The Move Ordering Algorithm

Let us stop first and examine the problem of move ordering. Since the move generator we have described actually computes all the legal moves, we could theoretically produce them in whatever order we want. What does it mean for one move to be better than another? It means that the value returned by the search when making the better move is higher than that returned when searching the other move. This can depend on information that either is not available at the position in which the moves are being made or that is too expensive to compute, in effect requiring some sort of search. The move ordering must be made using locally available information that estimates how the evaluation is likely to be affected by a move, at least over the short term. The following are examples of short-term heuristics:

1. A capture raises the evaluation, and the expected increase is the value of the captured piece. Thus the moves to try first are those that capture the most valuable pieces.

2. Since there is a possibility of recapture, the evaluation may be decreased by the value of the moving piece. Thus the least valuable pieces should be moved first.

3. To avoid the possibility of recapture, moves to safer squares should be tried first. While safety is impossible to judge precisely without a search, an estimate can be obtained by determining which pieces for each side bear on the square.

4. If pieces are left *en prise*, the evaluation will decrease as a result of their capture. Thus *en prise* pieces should be moved first.

5. A move to a central square is more likely to increase the positional part of the evaluation since pieces near the center exert control over more squares than those placed near the edge of the board.

These rules interact since following one may require violating another; therefore those judged more likely to produce a better evaluation are given priority. For example, the refutation principle indicates that most refutations are
simple captures that are covered by the first two rules. Belle uses the first
heuristic to determine the destination square, and then the second heuristic
to determine which piece to move. This provides quick refutation for bad
moves by attempting the capture of valuable pieces first. Unfortunately,
pieces are often guarded and such captures can themselves be refuted. For
example, QxB is better than NxR if the rook is guarded and the bishop is
not. Moreover, when the non-capture moves are made, and most moves are
not captures, the only heuristic used by Belle is to move the least valuable
pieces first without regard to the safety of the destination square. Including the safety of the destination square would appear to greatly improve the
move ordering. The safety of the origin square is much less important. While
one wants to move pieces that are *en prise*, this information does not provide
much disambiguation among moves since there are usually very few, if any,
pieces *en prise*. In any case, the refutation principle indicates that the most
important moves are those that refute the move just made by the other side
and moving an *en prise* piece rarely does this.

Since our move generator has available all legal moves for each side at all
times, it is able to estimate the relative safety of each square. The safety
of a square can be thought of in terms of the pieces that can occupy the
square without loss through recapture. For example, if each side has a knight
guarding a square, it is not safe to move a rook or queen to that square, but
it is safe to move a pawn, knight or bishop. Thus the safety heuristic is
closely related to the moving piece heuristic.

Our move ordering algorithm assigns a priority value to each legal move
and produces them in descending order according to this value. Since the
relative values of the ever-possible moves depend not only on the piece captured on the destination square but on the safety of the destination square,
the ever-possible moves cannot be ordered statically but must be reordered
depending on the current position. However, we can show that the ever-
possible moves to a single destination square can be ordered statically since
both the captured piece and the safety information can be factored out.

The heuristics listed above are based on the estimated increase in the
evaluation resulting from a move. This increase is $C - RC$ where C is the
value of the captured piece, or zero if the move is not a capture, and RC is
the value of any subsequent recapturing sequence to the same square by the

		Opponent's Guards			
Player's		$P = 0$		$P \neq 0$	
Guards		$G = 0$	$G \neq 0$	$G = 0$	$G \neq 0$
$P = 0$	$G = 0$	C	$C - M$	$C - M$	$C - M$
	$G \neq 0$	C	$\max \begin{cases} C \\ C - M + G_o \end{cases}$	$C - M + pawn$	$C - M$
$P \neq 0$	$G = 0$	C	C	$C - M + pawn$	$C - M$
	$G \neq 0$	C	C	$C - M + pawn$	$C - M + pawn$

Table 3.1: *This table shows how the moves to one destination square can be ordered based on the value of the moving piece, M, the value of the captured piece, C, the value of the piece guards, G, and pawn guards, P. For example, if neither the player nor the opponent has a pawn guard (P = 0) but both have a piece guard (G $\neq$ 0), then the value of the move can be estimated as the greater of C and (C − M + G_o), where G_o refers to the value of the opponent's piece guard.*

opposing side. If the opponent has no pieces guarding the square then RC is zero. Otherwise RC is $M + Ex$ where M is the value of the moving piece which is subject to recapture and Ex is the value of any subsequent exchange. The Ex term is somewhat complicated, being based on the number and value of the pieces guarding the square. Since an exact calculation of this value requires a search and since any such calculation is bound to be inaccurate because of what is happening on the rest of the board, we assume that Ex can be estimated sufficiently well by noting the pawns and the lowest valued piece for each side guarding the destination square. Table 3.1 shows the computed values for the moves based on the first four heuristics.

It is clear that the guard information for a square is constant over all the moves to that square. With the exception of the case in which both sides have a piece guard but no pawn guard, a single equation applies to all the moves to a square for a given position, and this equation is of the form $C - M + \text{constant}$. The only variable is M and thus the value of a move is directly related to $-M$.

The case in which both sides have a piece guard but no pawn guard is slightly different because of the max operator. In this case, the move value is $C - M + G_o$, if $M < G_o$ and C otherwise. The only effect of this is to raise the value of all the moves of pieces with a value less than the opponent's guard. Thus the static ordering based on the moving piece remains valid.

While the moves to each square can be ordered statically, the ordering of moves to different squares changes dynamically based on both capture differential and destination square safety. The overall move selection is done by first selecting the best move to each destination square based on the static ordering and then choosing the best from this set of moves based on dynamic information. This can be done by assigning a dynamic priority value to the best move to each square based on the calculations of Table 3.1 and selecting the move with the highest value as the best overall move.

Partitioning the circuit by destination square allows the move ordering just described to be done naturally. Since the moves to the same destination square are ordered statically, a standard priority encoder is used to select the best move to each square. Since all the moves to each destination square are generated simultaneously, the pawn and piece guard information can be extracted by examining the moves for each side and noting the pawn capture moves and the lowest valued piece move. Partitioning by destination square also allows the destination condition computation to be shared among all the moves, as previously noted.

The guard information in the current implementation is only approximated. First, the number of pawn guards is not determined, only the fact that there is at least one pawn guard. Referring to Table 3.1, one can see that this can only change the value of a move by a pawn in those cases where there are two pawn guards and no piece guard. The second pawn can effect a recapture of a pawn on the third or fourth move. This situation occurs only infrequently and the move ordering is only slightly perturbed.

Of more importance is the way in which the piece guards are calculated. When a position is first visited, the first move for each side is generated and used as the guard when computing the value of the moves to the square. Since the moves are generated in increasing order by piece value, the guards are the lowest valued pieces that can move to the square. There are three cases in which the guards are incorrect as a result of using the first move to a square as the guard.

1. When the first move is a pawn capture, the guard is incorrectly taken as a pawn instead of the lowest valued piece and it must be assumed that there is no piece guard. That is, $(G_m = \text{pawn}) \wedge (C \neq 0) \rightarrow (G_m = 0)$.

2. When the first move to a square is generated, the guard is actually the same as the moving piece and it must be assumed that there is no piece guard. That is, $(M = G_m) \rightarrow (G_m = 0)$. This is also the case when the move is a pawn capture: $(M = \text{pawn}) \wedge C \neq 0 \rightarrow (P_m = 0)$.

3. The moving piece may be backed up by another piece that will guard the destination square after the move, but the guard cannot be seen since it does not have a legal move to the destination square until after the first move. For example, a doubled rook will appear to be in danger since the second rook is blocked from the view of the destination square.

The result of these errors in guard calculation is the underestimation of the values of the affected moves. Where the affected move is a pawn capture, there is no real loss to not seeing the guard since the net evaluation gain is greater than or equal to 0. In the other cases, while the guard information may be underestimated, the pawn guards are correct and this is the primary source of information about square safety. In any case, the majority of refuting moves do not have to worry about an opposing guard and thus are not affected.

3.1.4   Maintaining the Context of Active Positions

The α-β search traverses the search tree in depth-first order so that at any position the first move is made and its subtree examined before the subtrees of the remaining moves are examined. Since only the first move is examined at about half the nodes in the tree, the move generator should generate a move only when required. This means that the context of the move generator must be saved from the time one move is generated until the next move is requested, during which the move generator processes the positions in the subtree. The move generator context includes the state of the origin, destination, and sliding registers, and which moves have already been generated. The register state is restored automatically by performing inverse moves when the search backs up the tree, and since the moves to each square are ordered statically, only the identity of the previous move generated needs to be saved. Each square must remember which moves it has generated since

the moves generated by different squares may be interleaved because of the
dynamic priority ordering. As Hsu[15] has noted, if all the moves to each
square are generated in sequence, as they are in Belle, then only the identity
of the square currently generating moves and the move last generated by
that square are required to generate the next move. In our case, however,
each chip must keep track of the moves it has already made, and this is done
by saving the index of the move as produced by the priority encoder.

The priority encoder has been designed to allow a *mask* input to specify
how many of the inputs are to be ignored. The first move is generated by
using a zero mask, the second best move is generated using the index of
the first move as the mask, and the remaining moves are generated one at
a time by using the index of the previous move as the mask. This index
then is sufficient context to continue the move generation. Since there are at
most 80 moves for each side to any square, the index is a $\log_2(80)$, or 7-bit,
number, and a stack capable of handling a 40 ply search requires only 280
bits.

The current implementation of the move generator partitions the circuit
into 64 chips, one for each destination square. Besides the move computations, each chip contains a maskable priority encoder, a stack of move indices
for maintaining context, a PLA for performing the dynamic move priority
calculation, and a distributed voting circuit that is used in conjunction with
the other chips for selecting the move with the highest priority. The voting
is done by having each chip place the priority of its move on a bus that all
chips can examine. The chip with the highest priority move can recognize
that no other chips have a better move and identifies itself. The details of
the move generator chip are described in the next section.

3.2   Move Generator Implementation

The move generator was implemented by partitioning the circuit onto 64
chips, each of which computes the moves to a different square of the board as
described in the previous section. One chip was designed with the ability to
generate the moves to any square of the board and 64 copies used to construct
the complete move generator. Each chip is then assigned to a different square
of the board during initialization. This allowed us to take advantage of the
relatively inexpensive replication costs of VLSI chips. In so doing, there are
some inefficiencies, especially at the edge of the board where there are fewer

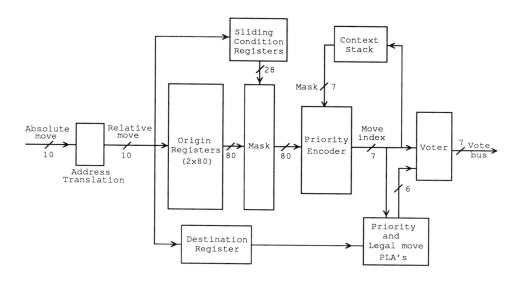

Figure 3.4: *Move generator chip block diagram.*

legal moves than at the center. While this particular implementation was convenient for prototyping the design, the move generator architecture allows a range of implementations using fewer chips or even wafer-scale integration to decrease board area, power consumption and delay. These implementation parameters will be discussed later in Section 6.5.

Figure 3.4 gives the block diagram of the move generator chip. The chip operates on a two phase clock with the operation to be performed during each clock cycle designated by a 5-bit command. Commands and data are broadcast to the chip array via two common busses and the chip outputs retrieved via a third bus. The output bus also doubles as a vote bus during the distributed voting cycles. The 64 chips are wired together in an 8 by 8 array with four chip select signals wired in such a way as to allow one chip, all chips or any subset of chips along any of the four rays to be enabled for an operation.

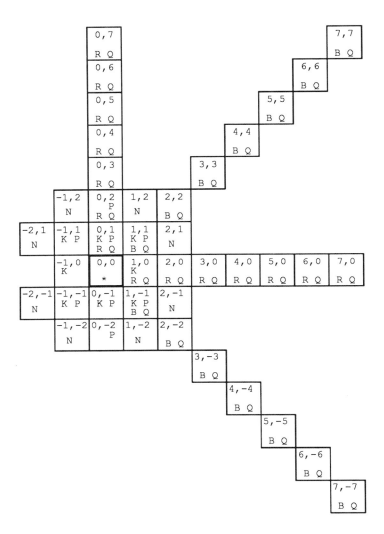

Figure 3.5: *The set of moves that the chip computes for each side.*

3.2.1   The Move Computation Circuit

Figure 3.5 shows the set of moves that each square must compute. Although there are at most 77 moves possible to any square, it is more convenient for

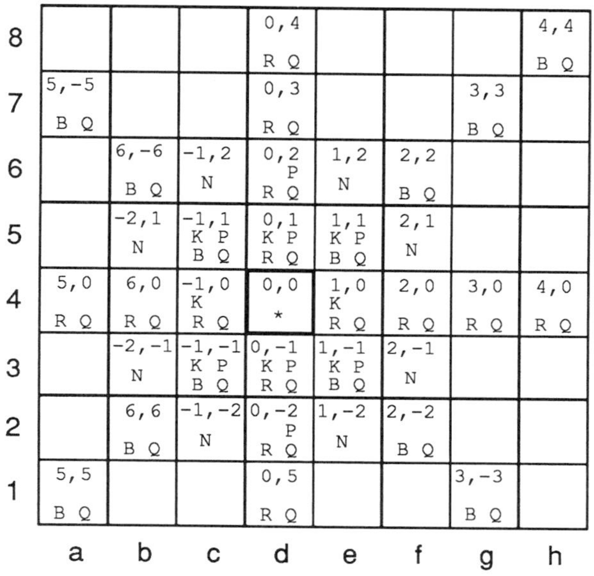

	a	b	c	d	e	f	g	h
8				0,4 R Q				4,4 B Q
7	5,-5 B Q			0,3 R Q			3,3 B Q	
6		6,-6 B Q	-1,2 N	0,2 P R Q	1,2 N	2,2 B Q		
5		-2,1 N	-1,1 K P B Q	0,1 K P R Q	1,1 K P B Q	2,1 N		
4	5,0 R Q	6,0 R Q	-1,0 K R Q	0,0 ⋆	1,0 K R Q	2,0 R Q	3,0 R Q	4,0 R Q
3		-2,-1 N	-1,-1 K P B Q	0,-1 K P R Q	1,-1 K P B Q	2,-1 N		
2		6,6 B Q	-1,-2 N	0,-2 P R Q	1,-2 N	2,-2 B Q		
1	5,5 B Q			0,5 R Q			3,-3 B Q	

Figure 3.6: *The move generator chip assigned to the square d4 maps the squares a4, b4, and c4 to the registers addressed by (5,0), (6,0) and (7,0).*

the chip design to assume that the 80 moves shown in this figure are possible. The destination square is assigned the address (0,0), and the possible origin squares are addressed relative to the destination address. The absolute addresses that are broadcast to the chips are transformed on chip into relative addresses by the simple subtraction: $(x_r, y_r) = (x_a, y_a) - (x_d, y_d)$ where (x_a, y_a) is the absolute address, (x_r, y_r) is the relative address, and (x_d, y_d) is the absolute address of the destination square assigned to the chip. Assigning a chip to a specific square causes each of the origin squares in the chip to be assigned to a specific square on the chess board. Figure 3.6 shows this assignment for the destination square d4 (absolute address (3,3)). For example, the absolute address (6,3) (square g4) is mapped to relative address (3,0). The relative address calculation is performed modulo 8 for sliding moves, in effect allowing the addresses of sliding moves to wrap around. For example, in Figure 3.6 the address of square c4, address (2,3), becomes (7,0) for sliding moves and (−1,0) for non-sliding moves. No ambiguity arises since only one absolute address can map to any one sliding move register address for

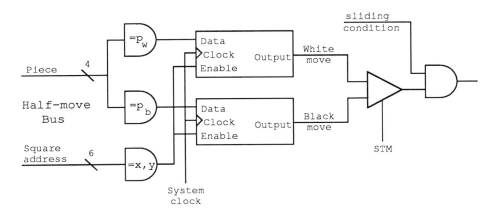

Figure 3.7: *The origin condition for one move for both white and black is stored in two registers. The output is selected based on which side is to move (STM).*

a given destination address. This avoids performing the two different move computations that a straightforward scheme would perform.

A single register is assigned to each of the 80 possible moves for each side. This register is set if and only if the origin condition is true for that move. When a halfmove is performed, each register that corresponds to the square specified by the halfmove may be changed depending on the piece and the type of the halfmove. For example, the halfmove that places a queen on the b3 square writes a 1 into the origin registers for all the queen moves from b3, of which there is at most one in each chip, and writes a 0 into the origin register for all other moves from b3. This means that the two halfmoves that are executed to remove the captured piece and place the moving piece on the destination square can be combined into one halfmove as far as the move generator chip is concerned since placing the moving piece automatically clears the captured piece.

Except for pawn moves, which are not symmetric with respect to the color that is moving, each of the 80 moves for one side is mirrored by the same move for the other. Thus the 160 registers are implemented as 80 double registers that share the same square address but recognize the opposite color piece. The circuit for one double register is given in Figure 3.7. The square address enables the register; a 1 is written if the piece matches the piece represented by the register, and a 0 otherwise. The output of the double register is selected by the STM input signal which indicates which side is moving. Since the registers are ordered by piece type, the circuit that performs the piece recognition can be shared by all the origin registers for one piece.

One may question the redundancy inherent in this representation of the location of pieces which is in effect a unary encoding. Perhaps a better representation would be a set of registers that contains an encoding of the location of the pieces. This would be cumbersome for two reasons. First, except for the king and queen, there is more than one piece of each type on the board, and it is an added complication to recognize which piece is moving. Moreover, in unusual situations caused by queening pawns, there may be more than the usual number of pieces of some type. Second, the decoding logic required to decode the encoded information would be larger and slower than that used by the move registers, which are small compared to the rest of the chip.

In Figure 3.5 it can be seen that there are sliding moves from 28 different origin squares and thus 28 sliding conditions that must be computed, each indicating whether a sliding move from one of the 28 squares is legal. These sliding conditions are computed separately from the origin conditions. The state of the seven squares in each of the four rays is kept in a set of 28 ray registers that are similar to the origin registers except that they are set if *any* piece occupies the square. Each sliding condition is then computed as a simple AND over the outputs of the appropriate ray registers.

The sliding condition computation is complicated somewhat by the arbitrary assignment of the destination address of the chip. As depicted in Figure 3.6, the sliding condition for a particular move register depends on whether the register is mapped to a square to the left or to the right of the destination square. In this example, a sliding move from address (2,0), square f4, passes through e4 on its way to the destination square. If the chip were assigned to h4 instead, address (2,0) would be mapped to b4, and a sliding move from (2,0) would pass through c4, d4, e4, f4, and g4. The sliding conditions are computed so that the move is allowed if it can move to the destination in either direction, but the location of the edge of the board is included in the calculation so that the move is always blocked in one direction by the edge of the board. The information about the edge location is part of the configuration information that is written to each chip during initialization.

The computation of the sliding moves is completed by AND'ing each of the origin conditions with the corresponding sliding condition. The result of

the move computation section is a set of 80 signals specifying the possible
moves for the side to move as indicated by STM. These moves are legal if
the destination condition, shared by all the moves, is met. The destination
condition is not included directly in the move computation since the information about which pieces bear on a square is required to compute the square
safety. This condition is used later to disable the chip from producing any
move if it is not satisfied.

3.2.2   The Maskable Priority Encoder

The 80 signal vector resulting from the move computation is produced in
descending order by piece value as described in the section on move ordering.
The priority encoder takes this vector and derives a 7-bit index corresponding
to the highest priority move possible. A mask input to the priority encoder
allows all moves with a priority higher than the mask to be ignored. All
the possible moves can be quickly extracted by starting with a mask of 0
to extract the first move index and then using each move index in turn to
extract the remaining moves. The time required to extract each move is
essentially constant, independent of the sparsity of the move vector. The
priority encoder is a two level encoder comprised of ten 8-1 and one 10-1
priority encoders with additional circuitry incorporated to implement the
mask.

3.2.3   The Context Stack

The depth-first search control examines the subtree below the first move of
a position before examining, if necessary, the remaining moves. The move
generator only produces one move at a time and each chip must remember
which moves it has already generated so that the next move in order can
be produced. This is done by saving the index of the previous move on a
stack that is pushed and popped as the search traverses the tree, with a
zero index indicating that no moves have been generated yet. The top of
this stack is used to mask the priority encoder so that all moves that have
already been produced are ignored. When making a move to a new position,
the chip which is producing the move replaces the top of its stack with the
index of the move just made, while the remaining 63 chips keep the previous
index. A zero is then pushed onto the stack of all the chips in preparation for
generating the first legal move in the new position. To return to a previous

position, a simple pop of the stack returns the mask to its former state so
that the next move can be generated.

The piece guards are also saved on the context stack since they remain
constant over all the moves in a position. When a position is first reached,
the first move for each side is taken as the piece guard of the square for the
move ordering calculation. Pawn advance and king moves are not considered
controlling moves and so the guard is set to NULL if the first move is either
a pawn advance or king move. To keep pawn advances from masking piece
guards, they are generated out of order just before king moves. In retrospect
this was a mistake since it often causes pawn advances to be generated much
later in the move ordering than they should be. A straightforward way
around this problem will be described in Section 6.5 when a redesign of the
move generator chip is discussed.

3.2.4 Dynamic Priority Table

The priority encoder selects the best move to a square based on the static
move ordering. This move is then assigned a dynamic priority value based
on the heuristics summarized in Table 3.1. This value is used to determine
the relative ordering of moves among the 64 chips. The dynamic priority
calculation is done by table lookup employing a PLA that uses the information about the moving piece, the captured piece, and the piece and pawn
guards to produce a 6-bit priority value. The piece guards are provided by
the context stack while the pawn guard information comes directly from the
pawn move registers for pawn captures. The priority of a king move to a
square guarded by the opposing side is given a zero priority, which can be
recognized by the controller to halt the generation of any remaining moves.

3.2.5 Distributed Voting

All chips select a best move and compute the corresponding dynamic priority
value in parallel. The chip that has the move with the highest priority is
then discovered through a voting procedure based on a 12-bit priority value
formed by concatenating the 6-bit dynamic priority with a unique 6-bit chip
ID that is used to break ties when two chips have the same dynamic priority.
The chip ID's are assigned according to the centrality heuristic so that moves
to the center of the board are produced first. The chip ID's can be reassigned

during a game if it is decided that pieces should gravitate towards another part of the board, towards the opposing king, for example.

The voting procedure is performed to eliminate all but the one chip having the move with the highest priority value. This is done by having each chip examine the priority values of all the other chips and eliminating itself when it finds that its value is not the highest. A series of up to four steps is required, with 3 bits of the value compared in each step by means of a 7-bit wired-OR vote bus used by each chip to assert its own priority and to examine that of others. The voting procedure starts by enabling all chips that have a legal move. During each step, each chip pulls down on the one wire corresponding to its current 3-bit value or on none if the value is zero. If the highest priority asserted on the bus is higher than that asserted by a chip, the chip disables itself, eliminating itself from further contention. Since the priority value is unique, only one chip remains enabled after four vote cycles. In the usual case where only a few chips have a legal move, only the first one or two cycles are required to identify the chip with the best move. To detect this situation, the chips are connected by a 2-D grid of vote status wires comprised of eight wires in each direction with each chip connected to one wire in the x direction and one wire in the y direction. Chips that are still competing in the voting sequence pull down on these two wires, and only when one chip is asserting these wires will just one wire in each direction be asserted. These signals are used to terminate the voting procedure when a single chip remains in competition. The coordinates of the winning chip are obtained by encoding the two unary numbers on these two sets of wires.

3.2.6   Destination Condition

The destination condition states that a possible move is legal if the destination square is not occupied by a piece of the same color. The state of the destination square is kept in a register that contains the piece on the destination square and this is updated each time a halfmove addresses the destination square. The chip has a legal move if there is at least one move asserted by the move computation and the destination condition is satisfied. This information is used to keep the chip from entering the voting cycle if there are no legal moves and is also available as an output signal called Any-Move. This signal is OR'ed over all the chips to determine if there are any legal moves at all.

If the destination register contains the king of the side not moving, and there is a legal move, then the Check output signal is asserted. This signal is also OR'ed over all chips to determine if a side is in check. When a voting cycle is not in progress, the vote status signals are used to locate the king in check. This king location information, which is required by the procedure that minimizes the number of illegal moves generated when escaping from check, is thus supplied by the move generator itself.

The quiescence portion of the search examines only capture sequences from a leaf position in an attempt to determine the true value of a position. A control signal to the move generator is asserted to indicate that only capture moves are to be generated. This becomes part of the destination condition in that the destination condition is no longer satisfied if the destination square is empty. This is not the same as stopping the move generation sequence after all captures have been generated since, unlike other move generators like Belle's, this one does not automatically produce captures first. Captures that are predicted to lose material are produced after safe non-captures and can be identified by examining the dynamic priority value. While one might think that these losing captures could be ignored in the quiescence search, they must be used since it may be the case that the piece moved was *en prise* or that the move makes a threat not recognized by the ordering heuristics, such as uncovering check. However, since other threats are ignored in the quiescence search, these moves probably can be safely ignored three or four moves deep into quiescence.

The question arises as to whether the moves are actually produced in descending order of dynamic priority value. If the dynamic priority of the moves produced by a chip is always monotonically decreasing, then the voting procedure ensures that all moves are produced in strict priority order. While the static ordering does imply decreasing priority values according to Table 3.1, in actual fact this ordering is violated for two different reasons. The first is that pawn advances are produced after queen moves and before king moves so that the piece guard is not masked by a pawn advance. The strict ordering is also violated because the guard information is not precise due to the way in which the piece guards are generated. For example, assume that there is a knight move and a rook move to a square guarded by a rook of the opposite side. The priority of the knight move should be somewhat better than even while the rook move should be somewhat less than even. However, the knight move looks much worse than even since the piece guard is a knight and thus it must be assumed that there is no guard at all. Although the moves are produced in the correct order according to their *real* priority since the moves are ordered statically, a problem is caused by the artificially low priority of the knight move: moves from other chips with priorities greater than the low priority of the knight move will be generated first. Measurements show that this does affect the move ordering, increasing the search size by 5 to 10%.

3.2.7   Move Generator Operation

The move generator is operated under external control in the sequence described in the following paragraph. The move generation sequence is embedded in the α-β procedure which may cause early termination of the procedure because of α-β cutoffs. The procedure shown begins with a position having been reached and before any operations have been performed to extract the legal moves. This control sequence is generated by an external controller that converts the move generator output to suitable halfmoves for driving the move generator and other modules. This controller also keeps the moves made when progressing down the search tree and provides the corresponding inverse halfmoves when backing up. We give the procedure with white to move.

1. Each chip computes the dynamic priority of its best move for white. Both the move and the dynamic priority value are latched by the voting circuit. If white has no more moves, control returns to the calling procedure.

2. The voting sequence is performed to determine which of the 64 chips has the best move.

3. The chip with the best move is selected and told to place its move on the output bus and replace the top of its context stack with the move index. The context stack of all chips is then pushed.

4. The move produced by the move generator is made by performing the two halfmoves required to update the origin and destination squares.

5. After white's move is made, the move generator computes white's moves in the new position. This in turn produces a signal indicating whether black's king is in check, which can be used to signal the controller to generate only black's escaping moves. White's first move is latched as its piece guard for the dynamic priority calculation.

6. After the STM signal is changed from white to black, all black's moves in the new position are generated along with a signal indicating whether white's king is in check. If so, white's move was illegal and this position is ignored by skipping to step 8. Black's best move is latched as its piece guard.

7. (This procedure is recursively executed in the new position with black to move.)

8. The search backs up to the previous position by performing the inverse of the halfmoves made in step 4.

9. The context stack of all chips is popped, returning the index of the previous move produced to the top of the stack.

10. The procedure continues at step 1 to extract the next legal move.

3.2.8 Special Operations

There are two operations that support functions that are not part of the normal move generator sequence. The first of these allows the move generator to be queried as to whether a specific move is legal, and the second allows the majority of illegal moves to be avoided when the side to move is escaping check. Both of these operations make use of an external move index specified from off-chip instead of by the context stack.

Move Queries   A move query is performed by computing externally the index of the move in question. This index, minus one, is used as the priority encoder mask when the next legal move is generated. This mask causes all moves with an index less than that of the move in question to be ignored. If the move is actually legal, then the chip at the destination square will latch the move as the next move. It remains only to select this chip and check whether the move it produces matches the queried move. This procedure takes only two cycles: one to compute the next legal move using the externally specified mask, and one to output the move and compare it to the queried move.

This move query capability is used to validate moves found in the hash table, allowing the best moves found during previous iterations to be tried first. Since there is a small probability of collisions in the hashing function used by the transposition table, not checking the legality of a suggested move could have disastrous results. As discussed in Chapter 6, using the hash table to improve move ordering reduces the search tree by at least a factor of two. Other optimizations to the search strategy such as the use of a killer table are also supported by this operation. In each of these, the next move to be tried is not produced by the move generator but by a cache of some sort. When making a move that is not produced by the move generator, the chips all push their current move index since no chip's move is being made. If the move does not produce a cutoff, the move will be made a second time when it is produced by the move generator in its normal sequence, but since the result of its subtree will have been stored in the hash table when it was searched the first time, only the cost of a single position is incurred and not that of the entire subtree.

Escaping Check   The second special operation allows one to start the move generation with a specific move instead of with the first pawn move as usual. The intended use of this operation is to allow the masking of illegal moves when escaping check. While the cost of making an illegal move is slight, only that of making the move and then unmaking it, measurements have shown that in many tactical positions there are more illegal moves made than legal moves. This effect is more of a factor for deep searches and is accentuated by the search algorithm decision to prolong searches that involve checks.

   When the king is in check, the only moves that can possibly be legal are king moves, the capture of the attacking piece, or the interposition of a piece between the attacker and the king if the attacker is a sliding piece. A king move may still be illegal if it moves to a square controlled by the opponent, but these illegal moves are given a priority of zero by the move generator and can be masked by terminating the move generation when the priority value reaches zero. The legal non-king moves can be described as moves to squares between the king and the attacking piece, including the square of the attacker. If the attacker is a knight, then only the knight's square is 'between' the knight and the king. This does not exclude all illegal moves: there may be more than one attacker so that interposition is ineffective, or the move may discover another check. However, this does exclude the vast majority of the illegal moves that would otherwise be generated. The move generator can be operated in such a way as to eliminate this set of illegal moves by instructing those chips at squares not between the king and the

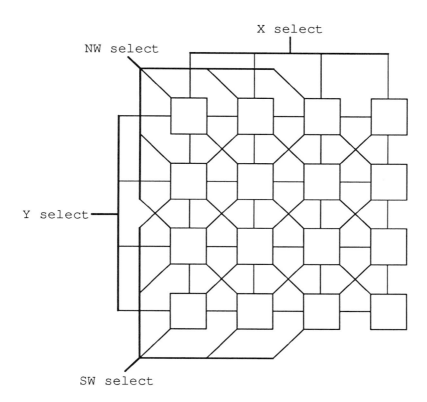

Figure 3.8: *The chip select signals connect the array in each of the four ray directions.*

attacker to generate only king moves.

The operation that supports this allows the top of stack to be set to an arbitrary value, in this case the index of the move prior to the first king move. Since king moves are the last to be generated, all other piece moves are masked by this index. When this operation is executed, selected chips write a zero to the top of the context stack while unselected chips write the external index. To mask illegal moves, this operation is executed with the chips on the ray between the king and the attacker inclusive selected before the normal move generation process is begun.

The following sequence of operations replaces the normal stack push operation when a position requiring an escape from check is first entered. This is shown for white in check.

1. The side to move signal is changed to black and the location of the white king is determined using the vote status signals.

2. Black's legal moves are computed by each chip.

3. The white king's square is selected and black's first move to that square is generated. This identifies the location of an attacking piece.

4. The chips between the source and destination of black's move, including the origin square, are selected and the top of the stack of unselected chips is replaced by the index of the first king move.

5. The side to move signal is changed back to white and the normal move generation sequence is started.

The selection of any set of chips along a ray is made possible by four chip enable inputs on each chip, one for each of the four ray directions. Chip select wires are connected to the chip enables of each chip in the array as shown in Figure 3.8. Each select wire corresponds to one ray on the board, with eight in each of the horizontal and vertical directions and 13 in each of the diagonal directions. A chip is selected if any two of the four chip enable signals are asserted. All chips are selected by asserting all enable signals in the horizontal and vertical directions, one chip is selected by asserting the appropriate enable in the horizontal and vertical directions, and a ray of chips is enabled by asserting the appropriate enable in the direction of the ray and a subset of the enables in a perpendicular direction. This enable generation is performed by table lookup based on the location of the attacking piece and the king.

3.2.9   Chip Initialization and Testing

A shift register links all the registers on the chip, including those that are used to assign a chip to a destination square. This includes the destination address that is used to convert absolute addresses to relative addresses, the registers that indicate the edge of the board for the sliding condition computation, and the chip ID register. Initialization information is loaded into the move generator array via the shift register, and testing and debugging are performed by comparing the data in the shift register to what should be there. The initialization of all 64 chips via the shift register takes a few seconds, but this is done only when the host program is loaded and initializes the hardware as part of its start up sequence.

4

Position Evaluation

The third component of the classic chess program that goes along with the search control and move generation is position evaluation. In theory, the search terminates only at nodes whose values are win, loss or draw, but such a termination condition cannot be used in practice since complete game trees for most interesting positions consist of at least 10^{100} nodes. The evaluation function is used to approximate the result of a complete search by computing values by which different positions can be compared. Each leaf node, as determined by some *a priori* depth limitation, is assigned a value by the evaluation function to indicate the probable outcome of a complete search from that position. If one position is assigned a greater value than another, then it has a greater likelihood of resulting in a win. The higher the value, the greater the likelihood of a win. This definition of the evaluation follows the same intuitive idea that chess players use when describing a player as being a pawn ahead or a knight ahead. While the player may not win, he has a much better chance of winning if he is a pawn ahead than when the material is even, and an even better chance if he is a knight ahead. While material is the most important consideration, many more subtle factors arise when comparing positions since a winning position can be created without any win of material. An evaluation function that does not recognize these *positional* factors is sure to lose, even to an average player, given the search depths presently feasible.

4.1 Introduction

If one examines a typical winning line of play in a game between good players, there is a gradual progression from an even position to the final win. At first the advantage is subtle with one player having a positional advantage because his pieces are deployed more effectively than his opponent's. As the game progresses, this positional advantage is increased until at some point the player actually establishes a material advantage. Eventually the winning player is able to use his superior forces to engineer a mate. Positions in which the material balance is at stake are called *tactical* while those in which the players are jockeying for a positional advantage are called *positional*.

Positional factors in the evaluation can be thought of as corrections to the material factors. Each piece has an intrinsic value that may or may not be realized in a position depending on how well it is placed with respect to other pieces. For example, if a rook is in a position where it cannot contribute to either offense or defense, then it must be devalued to reflect its reduced effectiveness. In general the various positional factors measure the different ways that pieces work together and how they should be placed to maximize their effectiveness.

Computers tend to be very good at tactical play since the material computation is very simple and the deep search is often more than a human player can manage. It is in computing the subtle positional factors that computers have difficulty. Computers often use their superior tactical ability to save weak positions that were reached because of an inadequate understanding of the positional defects of earlier decisions. The problem is that these positional defects manifest themselves only after many moves so that no reasonable search can hope to discover their eventual effect. As more than one program has discovered, the only advantage that a deep search has in these cases is that the positional problem becomes apparent somewhat sooner, with only a slightly better chance of survival.

Evaluation, then, comprises many different factors, all of which must be taken into consideration when comparing two positions. While it is possible to carry the result of this evaluation as a vector of values, each representing some component of the evaluation, the values are typically combined into a simple scalar that represents the weighted sum of the components. These weights are assigned according to the relative importance of each component[24]. Choosing the correct weights is difficult because components may be more or less important depending on the exact position. In these cases, a correct evaluation requires that the weights be themselves the result of some 'higher-level' evaluation. These dynamically computed weights are called *application coefficients*[6].

The problem of combining the evaluation components into one scalar is difficult even for human players, involving decisions such as what constitutes sufficient positional compensation for some loss of material. How the application coefficients are computed is a matter of judgement and experience. We will assume initially that the components are evaluated in isolation and summed according to some *a priori* weights and later discuss how this assumption might be removed through a higher level evaluation that computes application coefficients.

4.1.1   Evaluation Values as Probabilities

The α-β search places absolute faith in the value that the evaluation function produces when choosing between different lines of play, ignoring the probabilities implicit in the values. The implications of this are discussed by Palay[22], who presents a search algorithm called PB* which assigns probability distributions to values instead of simple scalars. This is an extension of the B* search described by Berliner[3] which uses *ranges* instead of point values to take into account the uncertainty of the evaluation function. The actual value of a position is assumed to lie within the range returned by the evaluation function. Both these algorithms represent alternatives to the search control and not to the evaluation function itself. That is, leaf positions must be evaluated according to the same criteria, but the results are interpreted somewhat differently since it is recognized that there is a degree of uncertainty in the evaluation itself. In that sense, we ignore the issue of how the values produced by the evaluation function are used and concentrate only on how the evaluation function actually evaluates a position. Hitech currently uses a straight α-β search control, but its design does not preclude a more sophisticated search algorithm.

4.1.2   The Effect of Deep Search

There is a complex relationship between the evaluation function and the depth of search. As the search is able to see deeper, the evaluation function needs to know less about tactical factors other than simple material. For example, a capture is discovered by a one ply search which knows only about material, the concept of a fork is discovered by a three ply search, and the threat of a fork by a five ply search. Thus the evaluation function used by an eight ply search has less need to know explicitly about a fork than a six ply search. It has also been observed that pins, which are tactical in nature, become less of a problem when searching to eight ply than to six ply where the evaluation function must be aware of them[29]. In fact, Hitech does not understand the concept of pins but does not appear to suffer greatly from this fact. It may be that at advanced levels of play this will become a deficiency which must be overcome either by a deeper search or by explicit knowledge.

Other positional factors that have widely been thought to be important appear to be less important when searching deeply. Board control and piece mobility, two closely related positional factors, were mentioned in Shannon's original essay on computer chess[26]. While it is true that these are important concepts, a deep search often sees far enough ahead to discover the implications of good or bad board control and mobility[5]. Here again, Hitech has no direct measure of board control or mobility and yet rarely allows these to become a problem with its positional play. The key to building an effective evaluation function is deciding which factors are indeed important relative to the power of the search.

4.1.3 Designing an Evaluation Function

There are three related considerations involved with designing an evaluation function. The first is the identification of the knowledge required to understand positions sufficiently well. The level of play of the program ultimately depends on how well the evaluation function can distinguish good and bad positions. Identifying the components that the evaluation must understand is the job of an expert who knows the problem intimately and can identify and correct deficiencies discovered through experience with the program. The second consideration is whether these components can be computed efficiently, and this depends on the complexity of the evaluation and the power of the computational method. Finally, a decision must be made about which evaluation components to include in the final evaluation function. This decision must consider the tradeoff between search speed and the extent to which the evaluation should understand each position. This again is the product of the experience and judgement of an expert but also depends on how efficiently the evaluation can be implemented.

The tradeoff between search speed and knowledge is a classic one: including more knowledge in the search necessarily slows down the search. In computer chess, the emphasis has shifted over the past decade in favor of speed. In the last five years, the fast searchers, Belle and Cray Blitz, have routinely beaten the more knowledgeable programs such as NUCHESS.

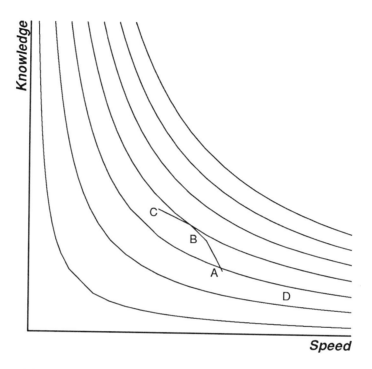

Figure 4.1: *The effect of knowledge and speed on search performance. The curves represent constant performance.*

This tradeoff can be illustrated by the graph in Figure 4.1 described by Berliner[2]. The curves indicate constant performance over a range of knowledge in the evaluation function and search speed. Any gain in knowledge must be balanced against the resulting decrease in speed. In many cases the amount of time spent analyzing some part of the evaluation slows the search to the point where the overall performance of the program suffers. The line ABC illustrates what may happen when some component is added to the evaluation. Adding a first cut approximation moves the program from A to B where the evaluation captures perhaps half of the knowledge with little effort. Computing the component more precisely in order to capture the remaining knowledge moves the program from B to C but only with a substantial speed penalty. The result is an actual decrease in the level of play. This explains why giving the program an overall idea of some chess knowledge often produces better play than trying to include the knowledge precisely. The deep searchers are currently in the vicinity of D where increases in speed alone is yielding diminishing returns. The problem is how to increase the knowledge without decreasing the speed.

4.1.4   Serial and Parallel Evaluation

The separate components of the evaluation may be computed serially or in parallel both across all the evaluation components and within each component. Some optimizations can be performed when evaluating the components serially. If those components that are most important are computed first, then in many cases an intermediate result is sufficient to force an α-β cutoff if the remaining unevaluated components cannot change the value enough to produce a different α-β decision. This method is used by Belle to skip the 'slow' comprehensive evaluation when a 'fast' evaluation produces a cutoff. Serial evaluation can also be more effective when evaluating each isolated component, if evaluating the information can be described as a discrimination process. That is, initial steps in the evaluation prune the amount of information that must be analyzed in subsequent steps to the point where the computation becomes efficient. The move generator provides a good example of the differences between serial and parallel computation. In the serial approach, each piece is considered in turn and only the moves that these pieces are in position to make are considered. Moreover, when computing the moves of sliding pieces, the moves are considered in order of increasing distance; if a blocking piece is found, the remaining moves along the same ray are ignored. By contrast, the parallel computation must examine all the ever-possible moves whether or not they are relevant in the end. The parallel approach trades 'wasted' computation for increased speed.

4.1.5   The Role of the Oracle

Another optimization that can be used for either serial or parallel evaluation involves the use of an *oracle* to decide which evaluation components are actually relevant in the region of the search[7]. The oracle is a separate unit from the α-β search algorithm and is invoked before the search is done to perform a detailed analysis of the root position to determine both which evaluations should be performed and exactly how they should be performed.

These decisions are made by looking at the root position and deciding the kind of terrain the search is likely to cover. In some cases this is straightforward. In the endgame, for example, the king shelter evaluation can be ignored. In other cases the oracle must make an educated guess, assuming, for instance, that certain pawn formations are unlikely to change. Using the oracle reduces the amount of evaluation performed in any one search, making a serial evaluation faster and a parallel evaluation more efficient in its use of hardware. This requires the hardware to be flexible so that it can perform different evaluations in different searches. The oracle also can decide how the individual evaluation components are to be valued, in effect tuning the evaluation function to the specific region of the search. This allows a more efficient implementation of the evaluation function in many cases as it need not be entirely general, but one geared to a specific situation. Again, this leads to more a efficient evaluation implementation.

The weakness of using an oracle derives from the assumptions that must be made at the root. If these assumptions are very far wrong, then the wrong move may be chosen on the basis of an incorrect evaluation. One way to reduce the possibility of error is to perform the oracle analysis not at the root of the tree but after each of the first moves from the root. While this is theoretically possible, there are two difficulties in practice. First, if the evaluation function used in each subtree is different, it is very difficult to make the values commensurate. Second, the oracle analysis is generally sufficiently complex that performing it thirty or forty times instead of just once is not possible.

The oracle and the search itself have different computational demands. The oracle is a complicated, continually changing program that performs a high-level analysis of the situation, but since it is invoked only infrequently, it does not need to be particularly fast as long as the analysis can be completed in a fraction of the time used by the searcher. So while the searcher is best implemented with custom hardware tuned to the α-β search algorithm, the oracle is best implemented on a general purpose computer with high level languages and support for symbol manipulation.

In the rest of this chapter we consider only parallel evaluation methods. Since the goal of Hitech is to reduce the time spent on move generation and evaluation to something comparable to that used by the search control, some form of parallel evaluation is the only alternative. We begin by analyzing the computational requirements of the evaluation function, then present an evaluation scheme quite similar to the move generator architecture, and finally discuss how some of the more common evaluation components are computed.

4.2   Evaluation Complexity

The different components of the evaluation function have widely varying computational requirements. We classify an evaluation function as first-order, second-order or higher-order based on its computational complexity. An evaluation function, $f(S)$, is defined as first-order if, and only if,

$$f(S) = \sum_i g(s_i) \qquad (4.1)$$

where i ranges over all the squares of the board in position S and s_i is the piece on square i. In other words, a first-order evaluation can be computed by examining the state of each square of the board independent of the other pieces and squares. Moreover, the overall value is computed as the linear sum of the values of the separate squares. This means that the function f can be computed incrementally during the search. That is, if the difference between two positions S^i and S^f involves only one square, δ, then

$$f(S^f) = f(S^i) - g(s^i_\delta) + g(s^f_\delta) \qquad (4.2)$$

since

$$f(S^f) = \sum_{j \neq \delta} g(s^f_j) + g(s^f_\delta)$$

and

$$f(S^i) = \sum_{j \neq \delta} g(s^i_j) + g(s^i_\delta).$$

Once the initial value of the evaluation function is established, computing its value at new positions is accomplished by computing the function g on the s_δ's that describe the difference between neighboring positions in the search. There is a close relationship between the s_δ's used here and the halfmove operators that we have used previously to describe the incremental change from one search position to another. A *remove piece* halfmove corresponds to the negative term in equation 4.2 and a *place piece* halfmove to the positive term. Since most moves affect two squares, a total of four halfmoves are required to move the search from one position to another. If $g(\text{NULL}) = 0$, where NULL represents the state in which no piece occupies the square, then only two halfmoves are needed for non-capturing moves, and three for captures.

The prime example of incremental evaluation is that of material evaluation which totals each player's material. In this case the function g is defined simply by

$$g(s_\delta) = \text{Value}(s_\delta)$$

where values are assigned to each piece based on their relative strengths. By contrast, determining whether a pawn is isolated cannot be done incrementally, since it requires information about the presence of pawns on three adjacent files.

A second-order evaluation function is one that depends on the relationship between two or more squares and thus cannot be computed incrementally. A second-order evaluation function cannot be described by equation 4.1 and must be described by the more general equation

$$f(S) = g(s_1, s_2, \ldots, s_k), \text{where } k > 1. \tag{4.3}$$

In the worst case, g may be a function over the entire board, but generally second-order evaluations depend on a subset of the squares. For example, each legal move computation performed by the move generator is a second-order evaluation. The legality of a move depends on the state of the origin, destination and possibly intervening squares. This second-order evaluation operates over a relatively small subset of the board state, which led to the simple parallel architecture based on distributed state described in Chapter 3. It should not be surprising that a similar architecture is useful for performing position evaluation.

We consider evaluation functions that depend on the *history* of the game to be higher-order functions. For example, castling information is not second-order since an examination of the current position is not sufficient to decide whether a player has the castling privilege. Other examples include the evaluation of repeated positions as draws and recognizing *en passant* captures. We will not be concerned with the computation of higher-order evaluation under the assumption that only a few are important, and these can be computed with specialized *ad hoc* methods.

4.3   Implementing the Evaluation Function

First-order evaluation is interesting since it is extremely easy to compute, requiring only the specification of the function g in equation 4.1. The domain of g is the cross product of the set of pieces and the set of squares. Since there are 12 different pieces and 64 squares, g can be completely specified by a table with 768 entries. Moreover, many different first-order evaluations can be combined into one since

$$f_1(S^f) + f_2(S^f) = f_1(S^i) - g_1(s_\delta^i) + g_1(s_\delta^f) + f_2(S^i) - g_2(s_\delta^i) + g_2(s_\delta^f)$$

and thus

$$g(s) = g_1(s) + g_2(s), \forall s.$$

Since it is so inexpensive to compute a first-order evaluation, it is advantageous to cast as much of the evaluation function as possible as first-order evaluation. Although at first glance there appears to be little besides simple material computation that is first-order, second-order evaluations can often be approximated by a first-order evaluation. While the result is less precise than that derived through second-order evaluation, in cases where the second-order evaluation is difficult to compute or not important enough to warrant the extra computation, the first-order evaluation can provide a performance gain if it adds any additional understanding at all since it does not slow down the search.

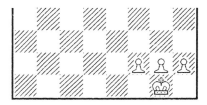

Figure 4.2: *The king is safe behind the pawns.*

As an example, consider the problem of king safety. In Figure 4.2 the king is safely hidden from attack behind the three pawns. Removing one of these pawns would put the king in some jeopardy, removing two would expose the king to serious threats, but removing all three would be a disaster. Advancing the pawns one square would weaken the shelter somewhat. This simple king shelter evaluation can be approximated by defining the function g as shown in Figure 4.3.

16	16	16
25	25	25

Figure 4.3: *The function g for pawn shelter as defined for the pawns on the six squares in front of the king, where a pawn is worth about 100 points.*

This definition of g gives the pawn shelter of Figure 4.2 a bonus of 75 points. Advancing one pawn loses 9 points, losing one pawn costs 25 points, and losing all three costs 75 points. Since the loss of the second and third pawn is much more serious than the loss of the first, a more precise pawn shelter evaluation would adjust the amount each pawn is worth *based on how many of the others are still present*. Moreover, capturing from h2 to g3 is much worse than advancing to h3, but this cannot be reflected by this first-order evaluation. However, the first-order approximation does give some idea about the value of these pawns, and while it is not as good as second-order evaluation, it is better than no evaluation at all.

The use of the oracle greatly enhances the utility of this type of approximation. The oracle analyzes the root position of the search and makes assumptions about the region encompassed by the search. This reduces the domain of the evaluation function so that the oracle can then adjust the first-order approximation to fit that part of the domain which is most likely to be evaluated during the search. For example, in the king shelter evaluation, the oracle can determine the relative values of the pawns based on the initial position. If there are only one or two pawns in the king shelter in the original position, their value must be increased to reflect the consequences of losing them. The definition of g can also be adjusted to make the approximation better at some points than at others depending on which cases are thought to be the most important.

The position in Figure 4.4 illustrates how this approach works. If a white pawn reaches the sixth rank or beyond on the a, b, or c files it will be passed. Likewise the black pawn will be passed if it reaches the third rank

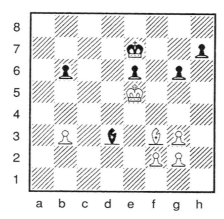

Figure 4.4: *The incremental evaluation can be used in some positions to recognize passed pawns.*

or beyond. Thus the incremental evaluation can be used to detect passed pawns by increasing the value of the pawns on those squares where they are sure to become passed. The incremental evaluation can do even better in this position if the values of both the white and black pawns are increased *anywhere* on the a, b and c files to reflect the fact that if either is captured, then the other pawn becomes passed.

Board control is another example where incremental evaluation has been used to capture some of the ideas of an inherently second-order evaluation. A complete evaluation of board control would require computing the legal moves for both sides and then deciding which player owns each square. However, the idea of centrality captures the fact that pieces near the center of the board tend to exert more control than those near the edge. Thus the value of a knight is increased if posted near the center and decreased if placed near the edge. The oracle can also redefine which are good squares based on the current board situation.

Using an oracle and first-order evaluation to approximate second-order evaluation yields surprisingly good play when used in combination with deep search. In fact, Hitech initially used only incremental evaluation in conjunction with an oracle, attaining an estimated rating of about 2000. But it would sometimes make serious mistakes because it did not understand some things about chess that involve second-order evaluation that cannot be reasonably approximated by a first-order evaluation controlled by an oracle. The primary deficiency involved some basic ideas about pawn structure such as doubled and isolated pawns. These concepts, which are crucial to playing high calibre chess, simply cannot be computed without second-order evaluation.

4.3.1 The Role of Evaluation in Strategic Play

Strategy refers to long term goals that guide one's play. For example, in the opening, one strategy may be to mount a king-side attack or to build an attack around a weakness in the opponent's defense, while an endgame strategy would be to try to queen a certain pawn. A deep search will often see far enough ahead to make plans of its own; strategy refers to plans that are so long range that the search cannot find them. Strategy can often be achieved through incremental evaluation[5,28]. For example, the oracle in its analysis may discover a weakness that it wishes to exploit or an angle of attack that it wishes to pursue. It can implement these plans by increasing the value of pieces on squares that further its plan. For example, it can pursue a king-side attack by increasing the value of its pieces on those squares that attack the squares in the vicinity of the king. Such a strategy is used in the assumption that increasing pressure on the opponent's king will create an opportunity that the deep search can exploit. A first-order evaluation works in this case since the king is not likely to move far within the search. Later in the game, when fewer pieces are blocking the path of the king and the search is deeper, a second-order evaluation may be necessary to relate the attacking pieces to the location of the king.

A typical strategy in the endgame involves queening pawns with the help of minor pieces and the king. In spite of their deep searching capabilities, computers often have no idea of how to proceed in such situations because long range plans are required. However, exact plans are not required, just some goal that leads the program to the place where it can see far enough ahead to formulate plans of its own. Typical plans involve knowing where the king should go to support its pawns or how to position rooks to give maximum support to their own pawns or to prevent the opponent's pawns from queening. Since pawns do not move very far within the search and the oracle knows which way they are going, a first-order evaluation can be used to indicate the 'best' squares for its pieces.

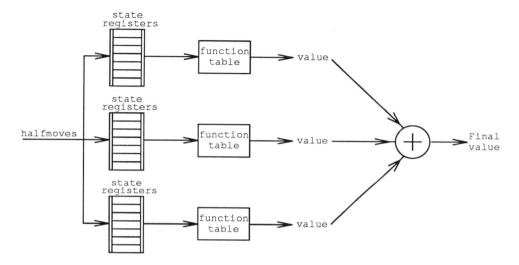

Figure 4.5: *The overall evaluation function is the combination of the parallel evaluation of independent components.*

4.4 Computing Second-Order Evaluations

As defined by equation 4.3, a second-order evaluation must be expressed as an arbitrary function over more than one square. Such an evaluation can be computed serially, as is usually done, but only at a cost to the search speed. The move generator has the same problem since the legal move computation is a second-order evaluation. This section describes an architecture for the evaluation function that is similar to that used for move generation. In the case of the move generator, each legal move computation operates on the set of state variables consisting of the origin square, the destination square, plus intervening squares for sliding moves, resulting in a boolean value indicating whether the move is legal. The state information for each move is maintained by a set of registers that are updated incrementally by halfmoves broadcast over the move bus.

In the case of an evaluation function, the computation operates over the state relevant to the particular evaluation component, and the result is a number representing the value of a particular state assignment. If the state over which the function operates is relatively small, then the function can be computed by table lookup. For the king safety example of Figure 4.2, the state can be represented as six bits, one for each pawn shelter location, and thus a 64 entry table is sufficient to compute the second-order pawn shelter evaluation precisely. This, in fact, is how Belle performs king safety evaluation[9]. In the case of a general second-order evaluation in which the relevant state might include the entire board, table lookup is not a feasible implementation. However, most evaluation components do not operate over the entire board, and those that do can be broken into sub-components that operate over some subset of the state and the results summed together. This overall evaluation architecture is summarized in the simple block diagram in Figure 4.5.

4.4.1   The State Variables

The relevant state for an evaluation component is maintained in a set of registers that is addressed by the halfmove bus in the same way as in the move generator. The design of the evaluation state registers as shown in Figure 4.6 is more general than that used in the move generator so that they can be programmed to represent a variety of different information. This programming is done by connecting the inputs of the AND gate controlling the register enable. When enabled, the register latches a **1** if the halfmove is a place halfmove and a **0** if it is a remove halfmove. This design restricts the use of halfmoves so that each piece must be placed or removed explicitly, unlike in the move generator where pieces are removed implicitly when a piece is placed on a square that is already occupied. That is, a place halfmove can be executed only when the square is empty and a remove halfmove only when the square is occupied by the piece specified by the halfmove. It is easy to make the search control comply with this restriction without incurring any additional overhead.

The range of interesting state information that can be encoded by this register is shown by the examples in Table 4.1. These examples assume a convenient encoding of the pieces so that information such as whether either a bishop or knight is on a square can be captured in a single register. These registers are really just one-bit up/down counters and as such cannot encode information about state variables that requires counting past one. For example, whether or not there is a pawn on either of two squares requires two registers; whether or not there is a pawn on a particular file requires six registers, one for each of the ranks on which a pawn can be; and counting the

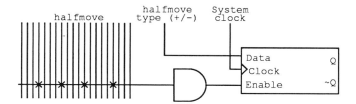

Figure 4.6: *The design of an evaluation state register. The information kept by the register is determined by which inputs are connected to the AND gate controlling the register enable. Connections are represented by x's where the input wires cross the AND gate input.*

State Information	Enable input		
	piece	**x**	**y**
White queen on square (2,3)	WQ	010	011
Any white piece on square (2,3)	W- - -	010	011
White bishop or knight on square (2,3)	W01-	010	011
Black queen on the board	BQ	- - -	- - -
White king on file 4	WK	100	- - -
File of white king: x_2	WK	1- -	- - -
x_1	WK	-1-	- - -
x_0	WK	- -1	- - -

Table 4.1: *Some examples of the types of state variables allowed by the register implementation of Figure 4.6. The information captured by a register is programmed by connecting the appropriate halfmove inputs to the AND gate governing the enable. Inputs that are not connected are indicated by –.*

number of knights on the board requires 64 registers. The obvious extension to this simple state register is to allow a larger count, two or three bits covering almost all interesting cases. Several of the simple state registers can be linked into one counter by including an enable carry term from the neighboring register as one more input term to the enable line. This revised register design is shown in Figure 4.7. This allows the number and size of the counter registers as well as the state information to be programmed.

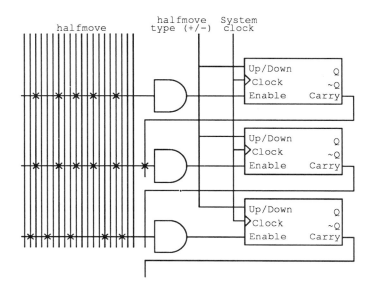

Figure 4.7: *A more general form of the evaluation state register allows several registers to be linked into a multibit counter for information that requires more than one bit of state.*

4.4.2 Computing the Evaluation by Table Lookup

In most evaluations the size of the input state varies from about 10 to 30 bits of information with the resulting values requiring a dynamic range of at most eight bits. A simple memory implementation is clearly impossible in general, but in most cases a PLA can efficiently implement a function of this complexity. The size of the PLA, measured as the number of pulldown transistor sites in the AND-OR matrix, depends on the number of inputs, outputs and minterms according to the equation $(2 \cdot \text{inputs} + \text{outputs}) \cdot \text{minterms}$. The factor of two results from the fact that both the true and complement forms of the inputs are used in the AND plane. Since a PLA's transistor sites are extremely small, PLA's with 64K transistor sites are easily implementable, although care must be taken to make large PLA's reasonably fast. If we assume that the largest size evaluation requires 32 inputs and eight outputs, then such a PLA allows over 1000 minterms, many more than required by the typical evaluation function.

If the oracle is to reuse evaluation units for different components and tune the evaluation depending on the search, it must be able to change the PLA's dynamically. Although there are field programmable versions of PLA's, standard PLA's are not dynamically programmable and are suitable only for situations for which the evaluation is fixed. Dynamically programmable, or alterable, PLA's can be built by embedding the PLA matrix in a memory array so that each bit of the memory controls one transistor site in the PLA. The memory can be either static or dynamic but can be simplified since the read/write speed of the memory is not important. Moreover, since the memory can be tested indirectly through the PLA, it does not need a read capability. An alterable PLA is slower than a standard PLA because each term in the AND-OR plane is connected to the drain of a transistor at each transistor site. This makes for at least twice as many drain connections for each product and output line, slowing the PLA down by a factor of at least two.

Marchand[17] describes a design for an alterable PLA that uses a three transistor dynamic memory cell to control each PLA transistor. This design uses a shift register along the edge of the PLA for writing, reading, and refreshing the memory cells. Since the refresh does not change the contents of the memory, it can be done invisibly while the PLA is in operation. Marchand also describes a chip that was fabricated to test this design. An alterable PLA with 22 inputs, 22 outputs and 64 minterms was built which requires almost 4K transistor sites. This chip was fabricated using a standard MOSIS-style NMOS process and measured about 5 mm.×5 mm., including the pads. The delay from input to output of the PLA was measured at 190 ns., which corresponds to somewhat more than twice the delay of a standard PLA of this size. A more aggressive technology and a larger die size would allow an alterable PLA with as many as 16K transistor sites with somewhat reduced delay. A CMOS PLA design using domino logic would be faster and dissipate less power than an nMOS PLA since the PLA output is generated only on request when the evaluation is performed.

The size of the evaluation PLA can be reduced if the PLA is made to produce an arbitrary default value instead of zero in the absence of any active product term. If this default represents the most common cases, the minterms to compute these values can be omitted from the PLA. Since the output of a PLA with no minterm asserted is zero, it can be made to produce

Number of inputs

8	10	12	14	16	18	20	22	24	26	28	30	32
341	292	256	227	204	186	170	157	146	136	128	120	113

Number of minterms

Figure 4.8: *The number of minterms computed by an alterable PLA with 8K transistor sites and eight outputs.*

an arbitrary value by XOR'ing this value with the PLA output and reassigning the values in the OR plane. If the number of state configurations that deviate from the default value is small, the size of the PLA can be reduced substantially. Figure 4.8 gives the range of PLA sizes that can be built assuming that 8K transistor sites are possible and that the dynamic range of the output is eight bits.

In our description of the state registers, we assumed that the AND gates were programmable without specifying the details. Since these gates are exactly the same as the AND plane of the PLA, they can be implemented in the same way as the alterable PLA. The size of the state register AND array is $(2 \cdot \text{inputs} + 1) \cdot \text{registers}$. With 10 halfmove inputs and 32 state registers this comes to 672 transistor sites for the register programming, adding about 10% to the size of the PLA. A block diagram of a general-purpose evaluation chip is given in Figure 4.9.

Although most of the evaluation components included in Hitech can be performed by this evaluation chip, there is a limit to the complexity of the evaluation that can be computed. In these cases the number of minterms exceed the capacity of the PLA. These complex cases can be handled by cascading the evaluation chips using the external inputs or by providing a feedback path for multiple levels of evaluation. This splits the evaluation into separate sub-components that are pre-processed to reduce the domain of the function. These sub-components are then combined using yet another second-order evaluation. This introduces extra levels of delay in the computation in return for a smaller circuit. This is analogous to using more than the minimum two levels of gates to compute complex boolean functions such as the parity function. The king safety evaluation is an example of this kind

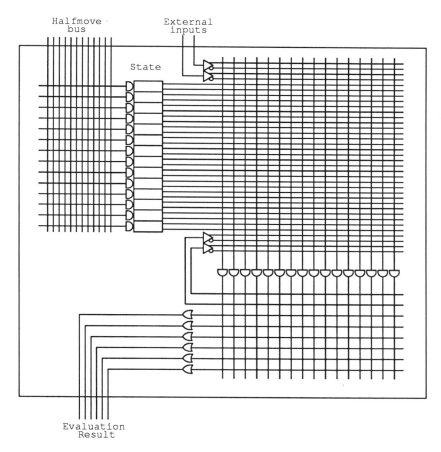

Figure 4.9: *A block diagram of the proposed general-purpose evaluation chip.*

of complex evaluation. This evaluation can be divided into evaluations of the pawn shelter, the presence of open files and the king location. This solution requires chips with external inputs for performing the final evaluation based on the results of the parts.

4.4.3   Combining Evaluation Component Results

We have assumed thus far that the results of several evaluation components are combined by simple addition. In this case the use of an adder tree allows the addition of N components in $\log N$ adder delays. This adder tree can be implemented externally or embedded on the chip although the total number of pins required is the same in either case. If static weights are used to combine the evaluation results, then they can be included in the values programmed into the PLA. Otherwise the application coefficient must be factored into the value either by making it another input to the evaluation or by multiplying the PLA output by the application coefficient, which is computed by an independent meta-evaluation.

The most common example of context that is used to determine application coefficients is that of material. For example, the weight given the king safety evaluation decreases with fewer pieces on the board. This is accomplished in the architecture described above simply by counting the number of different pieces, but the increased number of inputs and minterms required to weight the value may make the PLA unreasonably large in some cases. An alternative is to compute the application coefficient externally by a separate second-order evaluation and apply it to the evaluation using the external inputs. This introduces another level of delay to the evaluation, but allows a more precise evaluation. This is similar to the solution used to compute complex evaluations. Another possibility, if the application coefficients are small, is to actually multiply the result of the PLA output by the coefficient. If the size of the coefficient is restricted to only three or four bits, the multiplier can be included directly on the chip.

4.4.4   Evaluation Chip Parameters

The parameters of a general evaluation chip are the number of state variables, the number of external inputs, the number of minterms and the number of outputs. The size of the PLA, and thus the size of the chip, is determined by a combination of these parameters. A family of chips with roughly the same size but parameterized differently would provide the most flexibility. Since the output size can be fixed at 8 or 10 bits, the parameters that would be allowed to vary are the number of state variables and the number of external inputs. These and the size of the PLA would determine the number of minterms. A useful family of evaluation chips would have from 16 to 32 state variables and from 3 to 16 external inputs. More experience is needed with the types of chess knowledge required by the evaluation to determine which parts will be most useful.

4.5 Components of the Evaluation Function

We have described an architecture for general position evaluation and determined the range of parameters of a VLSI chip implementation. This section discusses some of the more common components of the evaluation and describes how they can be performed. While most of these can be done with general position evaluation, we also look into the specialized implementation required by some of the more complicated evaluation components such as board control and piece mobility that involve move generation and are thus much more complex than other typical evaluations. This section only outlines how the various evaluation components might be implemented and concentrates on the details of a general architecture that is broadly applicable to the evaluation function. We are primarily concerned with determining the kinds of evaluation that can be done; the precise details are beyond the scope of this thesis.

4.5.1 Material

The most important evaluation component is material. The combination of a deep search along with an accurate material calculation allows computers to play extremely good tactical chess. The material balance is computed simply by totaling the pieces for each side according to their relative value. For example, knights are generally considered to be worth about three pawns, bishops slightly more than knights, and queens a little more than a rook plus a bishop. Material evaluation can be computed incrementally by assigning the entries in the evaluation table $g(s_\delta) = \text{PieceValue}(s_\delta)$.

Piece values may change during the course of the game depending on the situation. For example, bishops increase in value as the number of pieces on the board decreases, while knights lose value. Such gradual changes can be made by the oracle since the values do not change greatly during the search. Positional factors that can be included as part of the first-order evaluation will be discussed in later sections.

4.5.2 Pawn Structure

Because the design philosophy of Hitech requires the evaluation to run as fast as the move generator and the search control, only incremental evaluation was included in the initial implementation. This version performed very well, mostly as a result of the oracle and the second-order evaluation approximations performed by a first-order incremental evaluation. But it became apparent rather quickly that there were some glaring deficiencies in the incremental evaluation that could be solved only by a second-order evaluation, and these primarily involved pawn structure. Not knowing the simple concepts of doubled pawns and isolated pawns meant that Hitech would often allow serious defects in its pawn structure that would turn a winning position into a losing one.

Isolated and Doubled Pawns   Isolated pawns are those that do not have a supporting pawn on either neighboring file. Doubled pawns occur when two or more pawns occupy the same file. Although it depends on the exact position, isolated and doubled pawns usually indicate a weakened pawn structure and their values should be reduced.

Section 4.3 discussed briefly the problem with trying to approximate the evaluation of isolated and doubled pawns. This failure accounted for much of Hitech's initial weakness. The information required to detect an isolated pawn or doubled pawns on a file is the number of pawns on the file and the two adjacent files, which clearly requires second-order evaluation. If we assume that there can be at most three pawns of one color on a file, then this requires three two-bit counters, or six bits. A table lookup of the evaluation function for isolated and doubled pawns on one file is then quite small, with only 64 entries. Twelve such units are required to evaluate pawn structure for the entire board, six for each side where files on edge of the board are handled by one unit.

A more precise evaluation can be computed if one has information about the opposing pawn structure. For example, doubled pawns may not be a liability depending on the way in which the opposing pawns are arrayed. This evaluation can be done by including the counts of the opponent's pawns on the three files in question and assuming that the pawn groups are facing. This allows the pawn structure evaluation used by Chess 4.5[28] to be approximated. Each evaluation unit now has 12 inputs, but only six units are required since the two result tables can be combined. This in fact is the pawn structure used by Hitech where the evaluation function table is implemented by a $4K \times 8$ PROM. To compute this evaluation with the proposed VLSI evaluation chip requires the same 12 bits of state and fewer than 300 minterms.

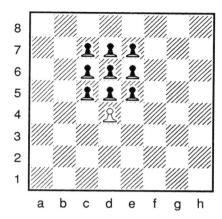

Figure 4.10: *The white pawn is passed if none of the indicated black pawns are present.*

Passed Pawns A passed pawn is one which has advanced far enough so that no opposing pawn can stop it from queening. Such a pawn is usually given increased value depending on how far it has advanced. Section 4.3 discussed how some passed pawn detection can be approximated using incremental evaluation and indicated the difficulty of recognizing pawns that become passed indirectly when an opponent's pawn is captured. A precise evaluation of passed pawns requires a second-order evaluation, and the simple count of pawns on the three files is not sufficient. As shown in Figure 4.10, the evaluation must examine a specific set of squares for opponent pawns. This evaluation is very straightforward, however, requiring only 21 bits of state, 15 for the black pawn locations and 6 for the white pawn location, and 5 minterms to detect a passed pawn on any one file.

In king and pawn endgames, a simple calculation can determine whether a passed pawn can be stopped by the opponent's king before queening. A pawn that is outside the square of the king, as shown in Figure 4.11, cannot be stopped by the king. The size of the square depends on the side to move, being one larger if the king moves first. This evaluation is clearly second-order and requires information about the material on the board and the location of the king. This evaluation can be done using 19 bits of state: 7 for the material count, 6 for the king location, and 6 for the pawn location,

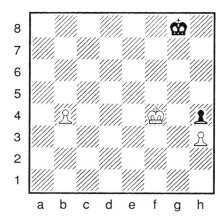

Figure 4.11: *If white moves first, then the pawn at b4 will be able to queen before the black king can stop it. A simple calculation can replace a six ply search.*

plus one external input indicating the side to move. The function itself can be computed with only about 50 minterms.

Until the game has progressed into the endgame, there is no reason to look for pawns that cannot be stopped. In this case, a complete passed pawn evaluation can be done with four evaluation units, each dealing with passed pawns of both sides on two files. Near the endgame, the four units would be switched to perform the more complicated unstoppable pawn evaluation for the four most interesting pawn files as determined by the oracle.

Open and Semi-Open Files An open file is one on which there are no pawns. Such a file becomes an avenue of attack for rooks and queens and can be especially dangerous if the file is near the king. A semi-open file contains an opponent pawn but no friendly pawn. Open and semi-open files can be either good or bad depending on the situation and how each player can exploit them. The detection of open files is used in conjunction with other information, such as the location of the king and rooks. Fortunately, the second-order evaluation to detect an open file is very simple, requiring only a count of the pawns on one file. This makes it possible to combine the open file detection with other factors, such as king or rook position, into one evaluation.

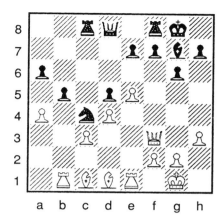

Figure 4.12: *The pawn on c3 is backward creating a hole at c4 on which the opponent has posted a knight that cannot be easily driven away.*

Backward Pawns A pawn is called backward if all the friendly pawns on adjacent files are in front of it and the square in front of it is not occupied by a pawn of either color. Since the pawn has been left behind by its neighbors, it cannot advance with support of another pawn and is thus vulnerable to attack. A backward pawn is even more vulnerable if it is on a semi-open file since it can come under attack by an enemy rook or queen. A pawn is very backward if the square in front of it is guarded by two opponent pawns. This means that the backward pawn cannot advance through piece support alone. The square in front of a backward pawn is called a hole and is a strong position for an enemy piece. Figure 4.12 shows an example where white has a backward pawn at c3 and black has posted a knight in the hole at c4. Incremental evaluation cannot be used effectively to detect backward pawns since it involves information about too many different squares.

A second-order evaluation to detect a backward pawn on square c3 requires information about the friendly pawns on squares c3, b2, b3, d2, d3 and any pawn on c4. Detecting whether the file is semi-open requires information about pawns on the squares c5, c6 and c7. Backward pawns can also be detected on c2 and c4 as well by sharing the state information among the three evaluations. An evaluation to detect backward or very backward pawns on any of these three squares, recognize a semi-open file, and adjust the value of any enemy piece posted on a hole square requires 29 bits of state

and about 100 minterms. Although a chess program may wish to detect
backward pawns on all eight files, which would occupy 16 evaluation units,
there are generally only a few files that are important, the two center files in
particular, and the oracle can assign just a few evaluation units to detecting
backward pawns.

King safety   Pawn structure is especially important in the vicinity of the
king where it is called the king shelter. Here the pawns should be deployed
in such a way as to keep the opponent from mounting an attack on the king.
Good players recognize from experience pawn structures that are good or bad
shelters. King safety becomes less of a problem as the amount of material
decreases since it becomes increasingly difficult for the opponent to mount
an attack. This is an example of a case in which an application coefficient
is required to change the value of the king safety evaluation as the material
balance changes.

The king safety evaluation must relate the location of the king to an
evaluation of the pawn structure. Castling causes a problem since the king
may end up in any of three locations, depending upon how it decides to
castle. If the king has not yet castled, then all three pawn shelters must
be evaluated and the results combined according to some estimate of the
king's eventual destination. This complicates the evaluation and also requires
external inputs indicating the castling status.

Incremental evaluation can be used to approximate the king safety evaluation as indicated in Section 4.3, but any precise evaluation of king safety
requires second-order evaluation to understand the pawn shelter and to relate it to the location of the king. In Hitech, the king safety evaluation on
each wing depends on the status of friendly pawns on about ten squares in
front of the king, the location of the king and the presence of semi-open
files near the king. This requires a PLA with about 20 inputs and several
hundred minterms. This evaluation is one in which several different factors
are detected and combined to produce a final evaluation. The complicated
part of this evaluation is in the categorizing of each of the different possible
pawn structures according to its sheltering ability. If the number of pawn
shelter categories can be reduced to a small number, then the number of
minterms required can be reduced by evaluating just the pawn shelter using
a separate unit and providing the result as an external input to the king
safety evaluation.

4.5.3   Board Control and Mobility

The intrinsic value of each piece is based primarily on the number of squares
it is able to control. This in part makes the queen the most valuable piece.
Board control refines the material evaluation by evaluating how effectively
the pieces have been deployed. This is done by measuring how much of the
board the pieces control under the assumption that pieces that are well placed
control more squares than pieces that are poorly placed. Board control can
be computed for each side as the sum

$$\sum_i w_i \cdot v_{p_i} \cdot c_i \qquad (4.4)$$

where i ranges over all the squares of the board, w_i is the weight assigned to
a square, v_{p_i} is the value assigned to the piece occupying the square, and c_i
is the control factor which ranges from 0 to 1 depending to what degree the
player controls the square. w and v reflect the importance of the square in
terms of its location—squares near the center of the board or the opponent's
king are more important—and the piece on the square.

Mobility is a related measure that determines how well a piece can be
brought into play. A good example of an immobilized piece is a rook trapped
in the corner by a king that has moved into the corner without castling.
Mobility can be computed as

$$\sum_p f_p(\sum_d c(d)) \qquad (4.5)$$

where p ranges over all pieces, d ranges over the squares to which the piece
has a legal move, $c(d)$ is 1 if the piece can actually move to square d safely,
and the function f_p computes the mobility value for the piece p based on
the number of safe squares to which it has access. Since the computation of
safe squares is very complicated, in effect an elaboration of the board control
evaluation, mobility is usually measured by counting the number of squares
to which a piece can move.

Board control and mobility are both very difficult to compute since they
require move generation for all pieces plus some computation of control based
on legal moves of each side to each square. We discuss how these can be
computed using a modification of the move generator described in Chapter 3
after examining some of the board control and mobility factors that can
be computed by a more straightforward evaluation. We put these under

the heading of general positional evaluation, but they have their roots in the ideas of board control and mobility. In fact, Hitech does not have any explicit evaluation of board control and mobility, and it is not clear that the additional evaluation effort would not be better spent elsewhere.

Centrality   Pieces are most likely to control squares in their immediate vicinity and thus should be placed near important squares. Since the important squares are usually those in the center of the board, pieces are best placed near the center. This is called piece centrality. Which squares are considered central may change during the game, but only slowly. At the beginning of the game the center squares are most important, but after the kings' positions have been established, one may wish to make squares near the opponent's king the center of attention. Centrality is clearly a first-order evaluation since it depends only on the location of each piece. Piece values near the center are increased and those near the edges decreased.

Rooks on Open Files and Doubled Rooks   Rooks are more effective when placed on open files where they can control an entire file and have immediate access to other parts of the board. The same is somewhat less true for semi-open files since an opponent's pawn blocks access into the opponent's territory. The second-order evaluation for detecting open files discussed in Section 4.5.2 is very simple and is easily combined with information about the location of the rooks to determine if there are rooks on open files.

Two rooks on the same file are referred to as doubled rooks and are especially dangerous if the file is open. This is just a slightly more general case of detecting rooks on open files. Since this evaluation is quite simple, two evaluation units can handle all files for both sides.

Explicit Board Control Evaluation   Board control can be evaluated explicitly by computing the sum in equation 4.4. Since the v_{p_s} term can be fixed over a search, each component of the sum requires the computation of the square control, determined by the set of legal moves for each side, multiplied by two weights, one fixed and the other determined by the piece on the square.

The degree of control over a square can be estimated quite accurately from the set of moves each side has to the square. The moves are computed for both sides in the same way as in the move generator except that sliding

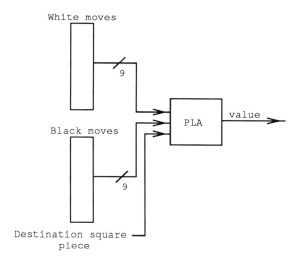

Figure 4.13: *The block diagram of the circuit for one square of the board control evaluation.*

pieces are blocked only by pieces that cannot move along the same ray. For example, if the rooks are doubled, then both exert control over the squares of the file. A pawn does not block a sliding piece moving to one of the two squares it controls and the king does not block a sliding piece moving to any of the squares to which the king can move.

As in the move generator, this results in a vector of 80 moves for each side, but these are reduced to nine signals for each side by encoding the number of moves by each piece type. Two are required for pawns, knights and rooks and one for bishops, the queen, and the king. The square control is a function of these 18 signals, and since the range of this function can be reduced to 16 or 32 values, the function can be computed by table lookup using a PLA. This calculation is similar to that used by the move generator to assign move priority but includes more information about the moves to a square. Depending on the size of the PLA, the weighting by the piece on the square can either be included in the PLA or multiplied into the result of the PLA.

The implementation of the board control circuit is much smaller than that of the move generator due to the absence of the priority encoder, stack and control circuitry. Current technology would allow eight squares to be included on one chip, for a total of eight chips for board control. A block diagram of the board control circuit for one square is shown in Figure 4.13.

Explicit Mobility Evaluation   Although the mobility evaluation involves the computation of legal moves, the structure of the move generator is not easily applied since it generates moves by destination square while equation 4.5 sums the number of moves by piece. Recall, however, that the move generator can be partitioned arbitrarily. Thus it can be just as easily partitioned according to origin square, where the origin registers are replaced by registers for each possible destination square and the origin condition is included along with the sliding conditions for each group of moves. The number of moves for each piece can then be tallied and the count combined with the piece type to yield a mobility value for each piece. This circuit is smaller than the one for board control, and only four chips would be needed to compute mobility.

4.6   Conclusions

Although we have not by any means exhausted the range of chess knowledge that can be included in position evaluation, the ones we have examined are the most common and demonstrate the range in complexity that is required. These include both first and second-order evaluations. First-order evaluation is important because it can be computed incrementally without slowing the search. When used in combination with an oracle to approximate second-order evaluation, it is a viable solution to position evaluation because it allows the fastest possible search at little cost. The oracle is the key to exploiting first-order evaluation to approximate second-order evaluation. By biasing the evaluation based on the root position, a better evaluation can be performed. This does involve some risk because the further one searches, the greater the difference becomes between the positions being evaluated and the root position.

   In spite of the advantages of first-order evaluation, there are many evaluation components that can be computed precisely only using second-order evaluation. Programs that do not understand these inherently second-order evaluations like pawn structure must rely on the deep search that the speed of first-order evaluation allows. It would appear that there is a wide gap between first-order evaluation, which takes no time at all, and second-order evaluation, which requires complex analysis.

We have been able to free the search from the tradeoff between speed and knowledge by using a generalized form of the distributed state architecture already used for move generation to do second-order evaluation almost as fast as first-order evaluation. Position evaluation is different from move generation because it is open-ended. While the moves that the move generator must recognize never change, it is not clear what knowledge should be included in position evaluation and how it should be used. As experience uncovers deficiencies, the evaluation must be improved to make it understand what it previously did not. This means that, unlike the move generator, the evaluation hardware should be programmable. This also makes the use of hardware more efficient, since the oracle can decide at each point in the game which evaluation components should be included, using the hardware for different evaluations as the game progresses. To otherwise perform all the evaluation that might be needed would require an order of magnitude more hardware. Thus the oracle has a similar role in second-order evaluation as in first-order evaluation, that of tuning the evaluation to the region of the search.

The depth of search has a great effect on the types of evaluation that are required. Many adages in chess serve to warn a player of the consequences of certain positional factors. A deep search can often discover these from first principles by looking at the consequences several moves ahead. In some sense, the deep search replaces the reasoning behind some of the more complex evaluations. The principles that are actually required by a deep search are the subject of continuing research. This power of the search to extend the knowledge in the evaluation was first discussed by Slate and Atkin[28].

That this evaluation architecture is effective is evidenced by the play of Hitech, a chess program that runs on special-purpose hardware based on this architecture. The combination of search speed and complex evaluation enabled by this architecture has carried its performance past that of any previous program. The power of this evaluation hardware lies in its ability to perform any number of second-order evaluations in parallel, with the results combined in $O(log)$ time.

5

The Hitech Chess Machine

The two previous chapters have described a parallel architecture for move generation and position evaluation, and presented a detailed VLSI implementation of both. Although these are the most important components of a chess program, they must be embedded in a system that performs the α-β algorithm and other functions such as repetition detection for the program to be fully operational. This chapter describes the chess hardware and software that makes up the Hitech system. Composed primarily of a full-scale implementation of the move generator and evaluation function that is the subject of this thesis, it also includes the software and hardware support to make full use of their capabilities. The performance analysis presented in the next chapter measures both the searching speed of Hitech and its chess playing ability. While we are concerned mostly with the performance of the move generator and position evaluation, these measurements are best done in the context of a fully working system. Thus it is important to understand the role of the other parts of the system and how they affect overall performance.

The importance of performing these measurements on a working system cannot be overemphasized. Extrapolating the performance of the system from limited experiments using simulation can be very misleading. This is especially the case when considering the role of evaluation with respect to deep search. Some evaluation components that have been generally accepted as necessary turn out to be much less important when using a deep search. Moreover, the experiments required to measure bottom-line performance—actual tournament games—require a fully functioning system. In the past, hardware move generator designs have been proposed[1,25] that are difficult to evaluate out of the context of a system in which they are used. Depending on how they are actually utilized, they may or may not be able to live up to the claims made for them.

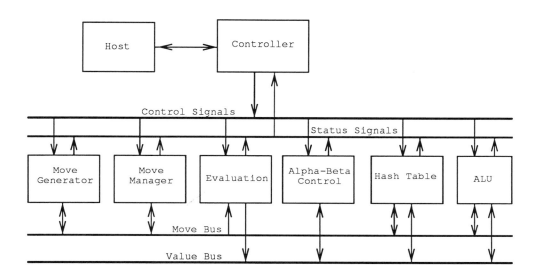

Figure 5.1: *The chess machine comprises a set of modules that operate under control of a microprogrammed controller and communicate over two shared busses.*

5.1 The Chess Machine Hardware

The structure of the chess machine, shown in Figure 5.1, is similar to that used by other special purpose machines like Belle[9]. A controller runs the α-β algorithm using specialized hardware units to perform the computationally complex tasks of move generation and evaluation. We have shown all the data manipulation hardware explicitly in this diagram, with the controller only generating control signals for the data units and determining the flow of control based on status signals generated by these modules.

Two data busses connect the chess machine modules. The first is the move bus, which communicates the halfmove operators used to move from one position in the search tree to the next. This bus contains piece, source and destination square values, each of which can be asserted independently by different modules. The second is the value bus, used to communicate values between the evaluation function and those modules that use values to perform the α-β decisions. Each module may generate status signals indicating the presence of specific conditions that are used by the controller to modify the flow of control. For example, the α-β module compares the value produced by the evaluation function to the current α-β values, generating two status signals that indicate whether the value is less than α, greater than or equal to β, or somewhere in between.

Each module operates in parallel under explicit instructions of the controller in the classic microprogramming method. During every cycle, each module executes the operation specified by the control signals generated by the current microinstruction. An alternative method would be to allow each module to operate independently under local control, synchronizing with the central controller only when necessary. This design style was not followed because we did not believe that the increased design complexity would be rewarded with a corresponding increase in performance. Since the α-β algorithm is so simple, modules would be synchronized almost every cycle. Moreover, allowing explicit control from a single microprogram allowed the flexibility required to implement different search strategies easily. The single exception to this was the design of the hash memory controller, which generates the memory chip control signals independently of the control program.

5.1.1   The Controller

The controller is a custom microprogrammed processor that provides control signals to each of the specialized hardware modules. A very wide microinstruction (160 bits) provides explicit control over every function unit, allowing maximum parallelism and flexibility in implementing the search algorithm. Experiments with different search strategies and optimizations can be performed simply by changing the microprogram.

The structure of the controller is shown in Figure 5.2. Microprogram control flow is specified by a next address field in the microinstruction. Branches are performed by OR'ing selected status signals into four bits of the next address field. By assigning branch targets appropriately, 2-way, 4-way, 8-way and 16-way branches can be performed based on any subset of the four status signals. Since this method of branching must reserve 16 addresses for each branch instruction, the use of a high proportion of branch instructions results in the under-utilization of microprogram memory. This was ameliorated by dividing the 31 groups of status bits selected by the branch condition field

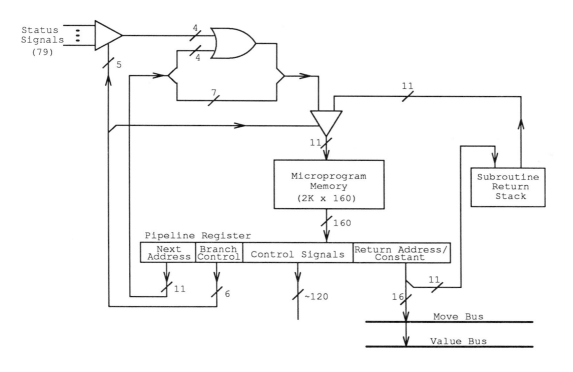

Figure 5.2: *The chess machine controller.*

of the microinstruction into two categories. The first category contains 15 groups that specify one status signal each, allowing 2-way branches with no memory overhead. The second category contains 16 groups that specify four status signals each for generalized multi-way branching. Although this allows 79 different status signals, in practice some common status signals such as the ALU condition code appear in more than one 16-way group since they are tested together with different status signals at different times.

Microsubroutines are supported by a subroutine return address stack. A subroutine call is performed by pushing a return address, specified by the return address microinstruction field, on the stack. Subroutines may be nested to a depth of 256 although in practice the depth rarely exceeds 50.

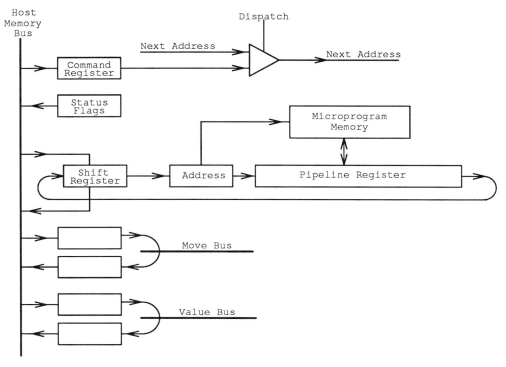

Figure 5.3: *The chess machine interfaces to the host via a set of memory-mapped registers.*

The controller interfaces to the host, currently a Sun-3 workstation, via an interface to the host bus, in this case the Multibus. This interface is shown in Figure 5.3. The interface contains several registers that are written and read by the host program to communicate data to and from the chess machine and to initiate execution of microprograms. Communication between the host and the chess machine uses a four-phase signaling convention. The host program indicates which function the chess machine is to perform by writing a microinstruction address into the command register. Writing the command register sets a flag in the controller that indicates it should transfer control to the indicated microroutine. When finished, the controller sets a flag in the interface informing the host that the operation has been completed. Data is passed between the host and chess machine via registers connected to the

move and value busses. Commands executed by the chess machine can be
thought of as subroutine calls by the host, where the arguments are written
into the move and value bus registers before writing the command register
and the results are read back when the operation is complete.

Microprograms are loaded into the microprogram memory via a special
interface register, which also allows the host to read back the memory and
verify its contents. Debugging is performed by modifying the microprogram
by inserting microinstructions that return to the host at those places in the
microprogram where a breakpoint is desired. This microinstruction places
the address of the next microinstruction on the return stack, allowing the host
to continue the microprogram after executing debugging microroutines that
access the state of the chess machine. The interface also contains a separate
profiling memory that counts the number of times each microinstruction has
been executed. This is used mainly to measure performance and tune the
microcode, but also to verify the operation of the machine when changes are
made to the microcode or to the hardware.

5.1.2 Move Generator

The move generator used by Hitech is built from 64 of the VLSI chips described in Chapter 3, with additional special hardware to generate castling
and *en passant* moves, which are not handled by the chips. The move generator chip control signals and timing are generated explicitly by the microprogram so that the chips can be tested easily by means of special debugging
microroutines. The four sets of chip select signals are generated by PROM's
addressed by the origin and destination square addresses on the move bus.
A microinstruction control field determines whether no chips, all chips, one
chip, or just the chips between the origin and destination square are selected.

The castling and *en passant* moves that are generated by special hardware
are only rarely legal and thus are handled as exceptional conditions by the
controller. If one of the special moves is legal, a status flag is asserted
which causes control to be diverted to a special routine that generates the
corresponding halfmoves. In the case of castling, the hardware asserts a
status flag if the player still has the castling privilege and there are no pieces
between the king and rook. The controller then queries the move generator
to determine whether the opponent controls any of the squares that the king
must cross.

Another special case is that of pawn promotion. Although the move gen-

erator produces pawn advances to the last rank, it does not perform the
actual promotion. This is done by special hardware that recognizes any
pawn move to the last rank and raises a status signal to force the controller
to intervene and promote the pawn to each of the four possible major pieces
in turn. Measurements bear out the fact that only a small fraction of the
time is spent processing special moves.

5.1.3   Position Evaluation

Hitech's evaluation is divided into three parts: an incremental evaluation
that is used in connection with an oracle as described in Chapter 4, a special
pawn structure evaluation that performs the evaluation described in Section 4.5.2, and general evaluation hardware that simulates the second-order
evaluation performed by the VLSI architecture described in Section 4.4. This
hardware comprises eight evaluation units, each of which keeps track of 22
bits of state information relevant to the particular component being evaluated. A function is computed over this state by a table-lookup procedure
that simulates the functionality of a PLA to produce an 8-bit value. The
results produced by the eight units are then summed together with the incremental and pawn structure evaluation to yield a final value. The state
representation used by each unit and the function performed is specified by
the oracle program before the start of each search.

The actual programming of the second-order evaluation hardware is specified using a compiler that allows one to define the functionality of each unit
in a straightforward manner. The evaluation function has evolved over the
past year and continues to evolve as more chess knowledge is programmed
into the hardware. The actual evaluation used by Hitech has been the work
of Hans Berliner and the details are beyond the scope of this thesis.

5.1.4   The Move Manager

The move manager is a simple data stack that saves the relevant information about moves as they are made and provides the corresponding inverse
halfmoves that back up the search to previous positions. Thus the search
alternates between using the move generator and the move manager as the
source of halfmoves depending on whether the search is moving forward or
backward in the tree.

When a forward move is made, the origin piece and square, and the destination piece and square are saved on the move manager stack, which is pushed and popped as the search moves forward and backward in the tree. When the move is to be reversed, halfmoves are constructed that remove the piece from the destination square, replace the piece formerly on the destination square, and replace the origin piece on the origin square. The move manager also maintains a copy of the current board position so that modules that supply moves need only supply the origin and destination addresses, with the move manager supplying the piece information.

5.1.5   The Transposition Hash Table

The hash table is an optimization that allows results that have already been computed to be used to reduce the search time. The hash table is used in two ways. The first is to detect transpositions, i.e. positions that are reached via two different paths in the search tree. By saving the result of each subsearch in the tree, the effort to search a position when it is reached a second time can be saved. The use of the hash table is complicated by α-β cutoffs that result in values that are bounds and not exact values. We maintain only one value for each position along with flags indicating whether the value is an exact value, a lower bound or an upper bound. In some cases it is necessary to re-search a subtree if the α-β values have changed since the previous search.

The second use of the hash table extends the usefulness of iterative deepening by using the information gained during previous search iterations to improve the move ordering. The hash table saves not only the result of previous searches, but also the move that achieved the result or forced an α-β cutoff. Searching this move first when searching the position to a greater depth yields near-optimal move ordering. If the move from the hash table is to be used it is imperative that it can be proved legal in the current position. If a hash table collision results in an illegal move, then the search and data structures are very likely to be compromised. Moves produced by the hash table are checked very quickly by the move generator using the procedure described in Section 3.2.8.

Using the oracle to change the evaluation function from one search to the next means that the *value* results from one search cannot be used in another since it is very difficult to construct different evaluation functions whose values are commensurate. Since the root positions of the two searches are different, the oracle uses different information when constructing the evaluation function. In general, the later search will use a more precise evaluation function, and using old values from the hash table may compromise the validity of the search and contradict assumptions made by the α-β search. Hitech currently erases the hash table before each search. An alternative approach would be to use the value results from old searches only in the first few iterations of the search, before marking all values invalid. If the evaluation has not changed, then this has no effect except to speed up the search. If the evaluation has changed, then the first search that does not use the old values from the hash table establishes the correct values. Preliminary measurements indicate that this strategy can result in a 10 to 20% speedup.

Unless one has a very large hash table in which all the positions examined in a search can be stored, a replacement algorithm must be considered. Hitech employs a depth-based replacement that does not allow the result of a shallow search to replace the result of a deep search. This has the effect of keeping those nodes near the root of the tree in the table. This algorithm is based on the fact that it is these results that are the most expensive to recompute. Moreover, move ordering is most important near the root of the tree where finding the best move or a cutoff is most expensive. The alternative replacement algorithm, simple replacement or FIFO, is based on the fact that positions are most likely to be repeated within a particular subtree and, moreover, that these repeated positions occur only at depth four or greater in the subtree. A comparison of the performance of these two algorithms is presented in the next chapter, and the depth-based replacement algorithm is shown to be better when the hash table is used both for saving results of earlier searches and for improving move ordering.

One way to obtain the performance of both replacement schemes is to use two tables. A secondary table is used to store in FIFO order those positions that cannot be stored in the main table. At the greater search depths, the main table becomes static as it is filled with positions near the top of the tree, and the FIFO table becomes a cache for nodes in the current subtree. Hitech approximates this behavior with a single table by restricting the set of nodes that can permanently occupy the transposition table. This is done by restricting the set of nodes that are subject to depth-based replacement to those within a certain depth of the root. These nodes are called *privileged* nodes and once established tend to remain in the table. The remaining entries in the table are replaced on a FIFO basis. Thus the hash table acts as a depth-based table for nodes near the root of the tree and a cache for the remaining nodes, except that non-privileged nodes that collide with privileged nodes are never stored. Experiments indicate that the privilege depth should be set such that only about 15% of the table is reserved for privileged nodes. This modification to the replacement algorithm reduces search times by 5 to 10% for middle game positions and by well over 50% for many endgame positions. More detailed results can be found in Chapter 6.

5.1.6 The Repetition Table

The repetition table is used to detect those situations covered by the repetition rule in chess: if a position is repeated three times, either side can claim a draw. The repetition table detects repeated positions by saving all the ancestors of the current search position in the repetition table. Some of these ancestors will have occurred in the game while the rest are part of the search. If a position is reached that has occurred previously as part of the search, including the root position, or has occurred twice in the game, it is scored a draw. This assumes that the search is deterministic, so that if a position occurs twice in the search, it will inevitably occur again. The repetition table is implemented using a small hash table with linear scan for collision resolution.

Both the transposition and repetition tables use an approximate representation of the board to reduce the number of bits used to represent a board position. A sufficiently large hash encoding using 48 bits is used to ensure that two different positions only rarely map to the same value[9]. The number of entries in the transposition table affects the search efficiency, but measurements show that the effect of the size of the table diminishes exponentially since it is the depth of the tree that can be saved which matters and not the number of nodes. The size of the repetition table is relatively unimportant as long as it can store all the positions of the longest game. Hitech's hash table contains 1024K entries and the repetition table 2048 entries.

5.1.7 The ALU

A general-purpose 16-bit ALU (AMD 29116) allows the microprogrammer to perform arbitrary computations on moves and values within the machine. The ALU is connected to both the move and value data busses, and condition codes generated by ALU operations can be tested by the controller. The ALU is typically used to experiment with modifications to the search algorithm. When the experiments verify the utility of some refinement, then explicit hardware support can be provided. Currently the ALU is used to discover recapture sequences and to implement the split hash table replacement algorithm.

5.1.8   Microprogramming Support

Microprograms are written in a simple language that is assembled into object code by a microassembler written in C. An excerpt from the Hitech microprogram is shown in Figure 5.4. Microinstruction fields that are not explicitly specified are given default values that are the most intuitive values for those fields. Microprograms are actually written as C programs using predefined macros as shown in this example. This allows the programmer to use the C preprocessor to define macros for certain idiomatic operations and to perform conditional assembly. The microassembler operates by executing the compiled microprogram to produce the object microprogram. The main work of the microassembler consists of assigning addresses to microinstructions based on branch conditions so that the minimum amount of memory is used. The microassembler also contains information about the timing requirements of the various modules and automatically generates the correct clock timing based on the operations performed by each microinstruction. In some cases it must rely on timing information given by the microprogrammer since it does not do any flow analysis to detect certain time-critical operation sequences.

5.1.9   Executing the Search

Figure 5.5 shows the operation of the hardware during the inner loop of the α-β search. This is an elaboration of the basic tree searching cycle that was described in the introduction. The details of the actual microprogram execution are given in the next chapter when the hardware performance in analyzed. They are not crucial to understanding how the hardware is used to execute the α-β search.

The move generation phase consists of computing the dynamic priority of the next move and voting to determine the chip with the best move. During this time the other hardware components are idle. Once the best move has been identified, it is made by executing three halfmoves. Although non-captures can be done with only two halfmoves, it is as fast to simply execute the redundant halfmove as it is to check that it is redundant. This making

```
Cycle (Search)
  Do(HashRefresh)
  Do(ClrMoveFound)
  Set(ConstantValue, 1)
  Do(ALUValueBus)
  AluSub1(DL, RHeight, RHeight)
  Do(RepWrite)  Set(RepCntl, REPSEARCH)
  Branch(NS,NS, EPLeft, EPRight)
    Case(0, SearchCastling)
    Case(1, EPMoveRight)
    Case(2, EPMoveLeft)
    Case(3, EPMoveBoth)
  EndBranch
End
Cycle (SearchCastling)
  Branch(NS,NS, KingSide, QueenSide)
    Case(0, Search3)
    Case(1, CastleQueenSide)
    Case(2, CastleKingSide)
    Case(3, CastleKingSide)  /* Try King side first */
  EndBranch
End
Cycle (Search3)
  Set(ConstantValue, MoveBus(0, 7, 0, 0, 0)) /* source file mask */
  Do(ALUValueBus)
  AluMove(DL, RMove)
  Branch1(PPpossible, TryPP, Search3a)
End
Cycle (TryPP)
  Set(MBSource, PROMSOURCE)
  Do(ALUMoveBus)
  AluAnd(DL, RMove, RMove)
  Branch1(STM, PPWhite, PPBlack)
End
```

Figure 5.4: *An excerpt from the Hitech microprogram. Each microinstruction as delimited by the* Cycle *and* End *statements specifies all the operations that should occur during one clock cycle. The* Cycle *statement includes a name that is used in the* Branch *statements of other microinstructions.*

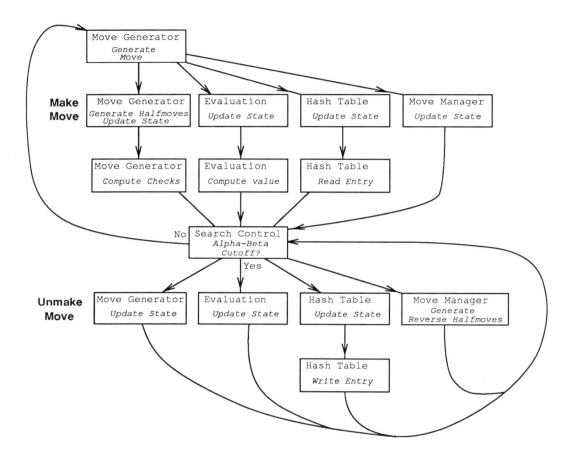

Figure 5.5: *An outline of the execution of the α-β search on the Hitech hardware.*

and unmaking of moves forms the backbone of the search. All modules that depend on the state of the search change that state when halfmoves are executed. This includes the move generator, the evaluation function, the hash table and the move manager. After a move has been made, each of the modules perform their different operations on the new position. The move generator calculates whether the new position is legal and whether the side to move is in check and the escape check mechanism should be invoked. The evaluation hardware computes a new value based on the new state, and the hash and repetition tables read the entries corresponding to the new position.

At this point, the search control decides whether a leaf position has been reached or whether the branch should be extended another ply. This decision is based primarily on depth and quiescence considerations, although the hash and repetition tables may provide an immediate value for the position. If indeed a leaf has been reached, the most recent move is reversed using information saved by the move manager and an entry is written into the hash table depending on the replacement algorithm. Otherwise the move generator or possibly the hash table produces the move with which to extend the tree.

When a move is reversed, all modules that maintain search state modify that state by executing the inverse of the halfmoves executed when the move was made. After the search backs up to a previous node, the decision is again made whether to extend the branch or whether the α-β criteria allows the search of the current branch to be discontinued.

The next chapter presents an evaluation of the performance of the hardware when doing the α-β search. That analysis shows that the hardware operates for the most part at the speed of the move generator. Allowing all the modules to execute in parallel as information is made available keeps the move generator constantly executing. Speeding up the move generator to match the speed of the other components would yield a speed increase of 30 to 40%.

5.2 Hitech Software

The Hitech software comprises a combination of a microprogram that performs the inner loop of the standard α-β search; a host program that performs the oracle analysis, time control and user interface; and interface routines that pass information between the host and the chess machine. The microprogram includes a standard quiescence search that examines all captures and responses to check. Moves that escape from check are not counted as a ply since they are considered to be forced moves.

Another example of a forced move is a move to recapture material after the opponent has made a capture, but one must be careful to distinguish forced recaptures from ordinary captures that are not direct responses to captures by the opponent. Our definition of a recapture is a capture that reestablishes the material to the level before a capture by the opponent. This definition includes almost all forcing recapture sequences. We approximate the detection of recaptures by assuming that the material level before the capture is the same as that at the root of the search tree, except when the opponent has made an unanswered capture, in which case it reverts to the root value of the previous search. We then redefine a recapture move as a capture that moves the evaluation into a window around the initial value. Depending on the size of the recapture window used, the search examines 10 to 25% more positions for a given search depth, but many problems involving forced recaptures can be solved. Whether extending lines of play with recaptures results in better overall performance is still open to question, but experiments conducted by playing Hitech against itself show it playing about 50 points better when detecting recaptures.

The oracle in the host program performs an analysis before every search and downloads information to the evaluation hardware. The host program then builds the first level of the search tree and orders the root moves using shallow searches to establish exact values for each position at the first ply. From there, the program does iterative deepening using the chess hardware until the time allocation algorithm decides that there is not enough time for another iteration. This algorithm decides how much time to spend on any one move based on the amount of time and number of moves left in the game and an estimate of the difficulty of the position. After a move is made, Hitech assumes that the opponent will make the expected response and begins a new search. If the opponent makes a different move, this search is discarded. The user interface allows the operator to set the game parameters, and entertains the operator with a variety of interesting information about the progress of the search including the current prime variation.

6

Performance Results

Hitech has achieved the highest level of play ever achieved by a computer and is currently rated at 2352, 150 points higher than the previous high-water mark. This places Hitech in the top 1% of all rated chess players in the United States. The progress of Hitech since its first tournament game in May, 1985, is plotted in Figure 6.1 along with the results of the rated games it has played. The steady progress exhibited by Hitech has resulted primarily from the continuous improvement of the evaluation function, but also from improvements to its opening book and some speed optimizations. Its current ranking relative to other rated players and programs is shown in Figure 6.2.

Hitech owes its performance to a combination of searching speed and knowledge. The speed derives from the fast move generator whose near-optimal ordering enables a very efficient α-β search. The knowledge is provided by an evaluation method that allows complex evaluation to be done extremely quickly. In contrast to other programs which have been subject to a tradeoff between speed and knowledge, these issues have been decoupled in the architecture employed by Hitech.

This chapter presents the performance measurements that indicate how each part of Hitech contributes to the overall result. Any such analysis of a complex system is difficult because of the symbiotic relationship among the parts of the system. For example, the transposition table and iterative deepening used together produce performance gains out of proportion to the gain produced by either used alone. Our approach will be to compare the performance of the complete system to that which results from changing or removing one of the components. This will isolate the effect of each component in the performance region which interests us.

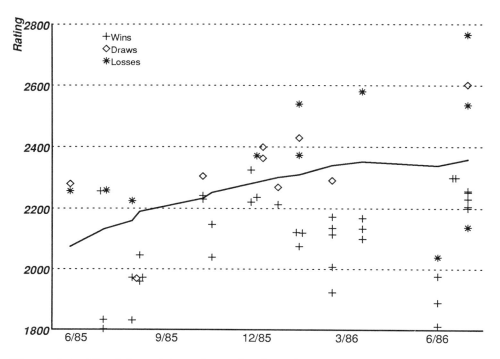

Figure 6.1: *Hitech's ranking, shown by the solid line, has risen steadily since its debut in May 1985. Game results against players rated over 1800 are also shown.*

Like other brute-force searching programs, Hitech is at that point in the speed-knowledge tradeoff curve where increases in knowledge produce greater performance gains than increases in speed. Before analyzing how well the hardware supports the searching paradigm that we have chosen, we first try to understand the role of both speed and knowledge in the overall performance of Hitech.

6.1   Search Speed and Performance

The performance of chess programs is often given in terms of the number of positions examined per second under the assumption that the program that looks at the most positions will be better. Speed measurements are

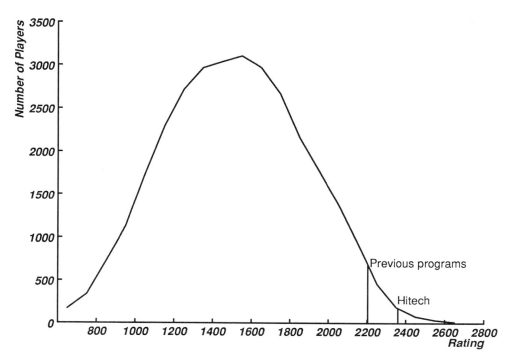

Figure 6.2: *The distribution of all ranked players in the U.S. showing the relative position of Hitech and the previous best rating attained by a computer.*

misleading for two reasons. Although the fast brute-force searchers have gained the upper hand in the past few years, a good evaluation function can make up for a certain amount of speed disadvantage. A good example of this is the NUCHESS program which plays better against human competition than Belle and Cray Blitz which outsearch it by one to two plies[2]. Second, a program may look at many positions unnecessarily if it examines moves in an inferior order. But it is true that increasing the speed of a program makes it play better, since by looking at a deeper search tree, it can find better moves. Unfortunately, a factor of four to five speedup is required to search just one additional ply.

Thompson[30] reports the results of experiments done by playing Belle against itself searching to different depths. These results are shown in Figure 6.3. It is questionable whether such experiments using a single program

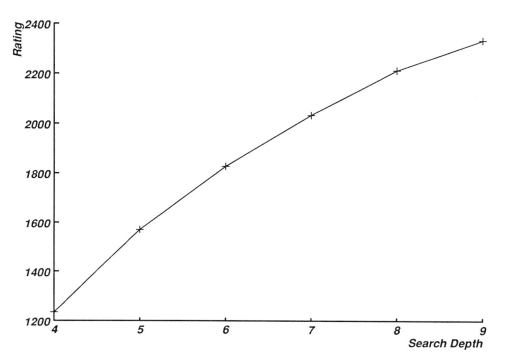

Figure 6.3: *The results of Thompson's experiment to determine the effect of speed on performance rating.*

can be extrapolated to performance against a variety of other players. It can be argued that the program with the slight edge in speed, in seeing slightly further, will eventually find an advantage that the other program cannot see, while the slower program does not have a hope of winning since it will never see more than the other program. In fact, the slower program sometimes wins since the game can drift by chance into a position that neither program understands where the slower program has the advantage. But since all the programs use the same evaluation function, this experiment is too sensitive to speed. Thompson notes, however, that the ratings determined by his experiment corresponded to Belle's actual performance when running at speeds between six and eight ply.

The slope of the curve in Figure 6.3 is about 150 points per ply in the region of an eight ply search, but only about 100 in the region of a nine ply search. If we assume that each additional ply costs a factor of four in time, then we can interpret this experiment to mean that each doubling in speed past eight or nine ply gains only 50 to 75 rating points. If anything, this overstates the gain to be had from increased speed. It is clear that the slope of the curve in Figure 6.3 is is steadily decreasing; using the same evaluation function for each program in the experiment makes it overly sensitive to search speed, and assuming that each additional ply costs only a factor of four is optimistic. Even so, we will use this somewhat optimistic figure of 50 points per doubling in speed to relate speed measurements to rating points.

6.2 Knowledge and Performance

Most of the 200 rating points that Hitech has gained since May, 1985, have resulted from increased knowledge in the evaluation. We estimate that to produce this same gain with increased search speed would have required a factor of 16 speedup. This conclusion is bolstered by experiments that were done playing Hitech in its present form against Hitech with no second-order evaluation except the pawn structure evaluation, which we will call Lotech. Hitech searching to six ply was able to play even with Lotech searching to eight ply[14]. This two ply increase in search depth represents a factor of 16 speedup. Moreover, the difference between the two programs appears to widen as the search depths are increased, an effect first observed by Slate and Atkin[28]. Although we did no experiments to measure the effect of the second-order pawn structure evaluation, experience with Hitech before any second-order evaluation hardware had been incorporated places its value at about 150 points for current search depths[8].

From these two sources of information, we can conclude that the path to better play for Hitech is through increased knowledge in the evaluation function. If one believes the knowledge-speed tradeoff curve described in Chapter 4, Hitech may reach the point where its performance is more easily improved by speeding up the search rather than by increasing the knowledge, especially as the knowledge becomes more and more complex. The remainder of this chapter analyzes the performance of the Hitech hardware, measuring how well it currently performs and indicating how it might be improved. We must keep in mind, however, that orders of magnitude speedup are required to make much difference in performance. It may be that advances in selective search will make such speedups unnecessary.

One answer that we will largely ignore is the technological one. That is, although one can obtain increased performance by using faster technology, for example by using ECL components instead of TTL, we are more concerned with architectural issues. On the other hand, we must ask whether our architecture for move generation and evaluation lends itself to faster technology, or whether they will become the bottleneck as other machine components are sped up. The fact that this architecture can be integrated over a wide range of circuit densities indicates that its performance will follow advancing technology. In other words, as improved technology is used to speed up the chess machine as a whole, the same technology can be used to make a faster move generator and position evaluator.

The performance measurements presented in this chapter fall into two broad categories. We first analyze the operation of the chess machine by measuring the amount of time spent performing the various functions such as move generation and evaluation. This is done by measuring both the frequency with which these operations are performed and the time required to perform them. These measurements give the raw speed of the hardware and also indicate those parts of the machine that limit performance. This will lead to conclusions about how the hardware could be changed to achieve better performance, and to an estimate of the ultimate performance of a machine using this architecture for a range of different technologies.

Next we measure the performance of the move generator move ordering by comparing the number of positions examined by Hitech against the number examined if an optimal move ordering were possible. Since the move ordering is greatly improved by the hash table, this analysis necessarily includes an analysis of the effectiveness of the hash table. We also compare our move generator ordering to other possible orderings.

6.3   Hardware Performance

The performance of the chess machine hardware was measured by profiling the search microprogram over a set of 28 selected tactical and positional problems to determine how much time was spent performing each of the search tasks. The results are shown in the flow graphs of Figure 6.4, 6.5 and 6.6.

These diagrams show the basic inner loop of the search, indicating the fraction of the total time spent performing each microinstruction. Each microinstruction is represented by a rectangle whose width represents how often the microinstruction is executed and whose height represents the time required to execute the microinstruction. Thus the area of the rectangle represents how much time the microinstruction adds to the total time spent per *legal* position. The fraction in the upper left corner of each rectangle is the number of times the instruction is executed per position and the tick marks on left side indicate the instruction cycle length in terms of 62 ns. subcycles. These are multiplied to give the total time contribution of the microinstruction to the time spent per position. This figure appears in the upper right corner. Where several microinstructions are executed as a basic block, these numbers are given for the entire block.

The total time per position adds up to 6,416 ns., of which 6,323 ns. are accounted for in these flow graphs. This corresponds to more than 150,000 positions searched per second. The actual number of positions searched by Hitech is somewhat less than this because of the time spent by the host software performing position analysis, time control and user interface functions.

The main functions performed by each microinstruction are given at the left of each rectangle where MG indicates a move generator operation, EV an evaluation function operation, and HT a hash table operation. The operation that constrains the length of the microinstruction is shown inside the rectangle. An indication of the length of the other operations that execute in parallel is given by a time line. It is clear that the move generator hardware is the component that restricts the speed of the search. In every case except those concerned with writing the hash table, the microinstruction length is determined by the speed of the move generator. The minimum microinstruction length in the current micromachine is about 180 ns., about what one would expect from LSTTL technology. The delay through the ALU, for example, is about 150 ns. The move generator is somewhat slower than the micromachine. If each microinstruction constrained by the move generator were reduced to the minimum length of three subcycles, the total time per position would be reduced to 4,672 ns., corresponding to 214,000 positions per second, a speedup of 37%.

6.3.1 Move Generator Operations

Some move generator operations are more easily sped up than others. For example, the voting cycles must be long enough for one chip to pull down the bus connected to all 64 chips and for other chips to respond to the priority

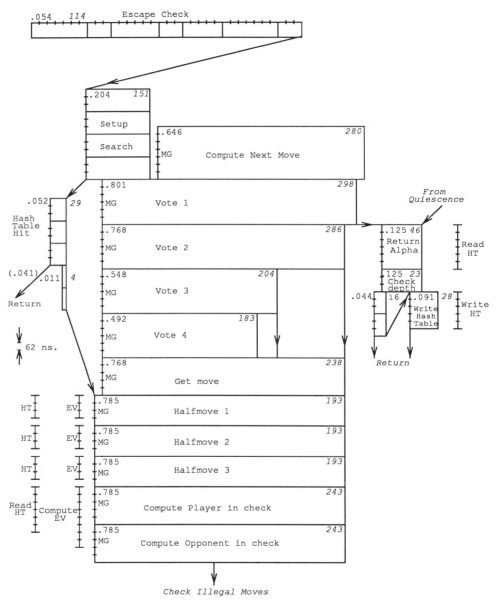

Figure 6.4: *Flow graph of the search inner loop: Part 1.*

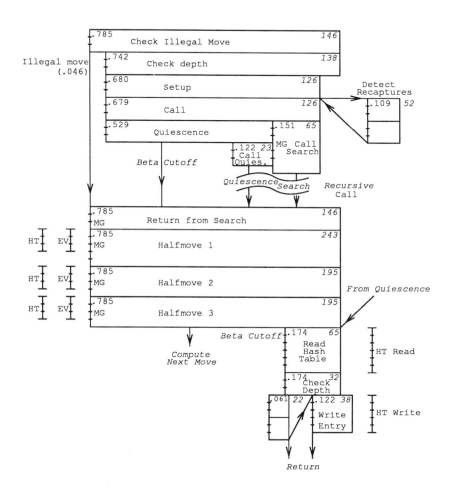

Figure 6.5: *Flow graph of the search inner loop: Part 2.*

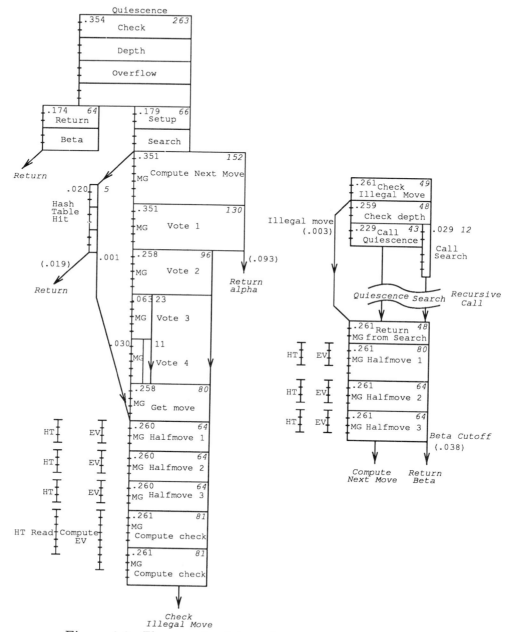

Figure 6.6: *Flow graph of the quiescence search inner loop.*

value, while the cycles that execute halfmoves are very fast since fast TTL
buffers are used to drive the broadcast bus. Figure 6.7 shows the amount
of time spent performing each move generator operation. We will consider
each move generator operation in turn, indicating where performance could
be improved without changing the underlying technology.

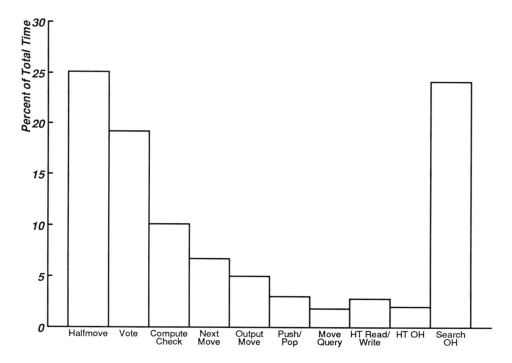

Figure 6.7: *The average amount of time spent performing move generator
and hash table functions for each legal position. Since the evaluation does
not currently affect the speed of the search, it does not appear in this figure.*

Execute Halfmove This function is perhaps the most basic in the search
inner loop since it is performed in unison with the other modules that maintain board state. In almost every case, this operation takes just one more
subcycle than the minimum three. The constraining factor is not the length
of the actual operation execution but the setup time for the data from the
move bus. By changing the timing of the move generator module, the length

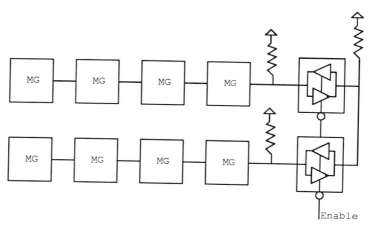

Figure 6.8: *External open-collector buffers are used to reduce the delay incurred when driving the vote bus.*

of the halfmove operation could be reduced to three, saving about 7.9% of the total time spent per position.

Voting The voting operation is very expensive considering that all the other modules are idle during voting and that so little work is performed. The time taken for voting is long both because of the number of cycles required and the length of each cycle. Each vote cycle begins with the vote bus precharged high. Each chip then asserts its priority by pulling down one of the seven wires. Since the vote bus connects all 64 chips, this requires discharging a substantial amount of capacitance. The time to do this was reduced by dividing the 64 chips into groups of eight and using open collector TTL buffers to drive the signals between groups as shown in Figure 6.8. A vote cycle begins with each chip pulling up the vote bus and the open collector buffers disabled. Next the buffers are enabled and the chips vote by pulling down on the vote bus according to their priority. When the voltage of any wire goes below TTL threshold, the buffers quickly act to assert the wires in all other groups. The voting sequence can be speeded up in two ways. First, better pads would allow the vote bus to be driven much more quickly. Second, the on-chip voting circuit is quite slow due to a carry chain used when computing whether the voter priority matches the bus priority. A simple look-ahead scheme using more circuitry would speed this substantially. It should be possible to reduce each vote microinstruction from six subcycles to three, halving the percentage of the total time spent on voting for each position from 19.2% to 9.6%.

Each chip indicates its voting status at the end of each vote cycle. This is used to terminate the voting sequence when only one chip is voting. This reduces the average length of the voting sequence from 4 to 3.10, resulting in a saving of about 5%. This optimization would have even greater effect if it were not for the one microinstruction delay until this status signal can affect the control flow. A circuit was included in the move generator module that recognized this status signal and changed the move generator controls appropriately to extract the next move instead of executing another vote cycle. Unfortunately, because of the difference in the move generator timing for these two operations, an extra subcycle had to be introduced into each vote cycle, actually resulting in slower operation, and thus this feature is not used. If this feature had been possible, it would have shortened the average length of the voting sequence to 2.55 cycles.

The average length of the voting sequence could also be reduced by assigning the dynamic priority values differently. Many moves are assigned the same priority by the priority PLA, requiring disambiguation using the chip ID. This is especially true at α_2 nodes where all moves are generated. Non-captures to safe squares are all given the same priority and thus require at least three voting cycles. This effect can be seen in Figure 6.6 which gives the details of the quiescence voting sequence. In 76% of cases, the first vote cycle produces a winner compared to only 29% in the normal search. The voting sequence could also be reduced by increasing the number of bits used during each voting cycle. Although the number of vote wires doubles for each additional bit used, the current implementation uses only 40 pins and increasing the number of squares on each chip does not increase the pin count. Current IC packages with more than 80 pins use about the same board space, so increasing the number of pins in return for faster operation is a good tradeoff. Using 15 wires in the vote bus instead of the current 7 would decrease the maximum number of vote cycles from four to three. In Section 6.5, we propose a way to reduce voting to a single cycle without sacrificing the effectiveness of the move ordering, in part by increasing the number of pins used for voting.

Output Move   During this operation a single chip drives its move onto the output bus. The length of this operation is determined almost completely by the time required to drive the output bus which is connected to all 64 chips. This problem has been discussed with respect to voting, and the solution discussed there using faster output pads would be applicable to this operation. This would reduce the overall search by about 2.0%.

Latch Guards/Compute Check This operation must be executed after each move is made to detect illegal moves or positions where the king must escape check. This incurs substantial delay considering how little information is computed. It is not the latching of the guards that is the constraining factor, but the delay until the InCheck signal becomes valid. This bottleneck was not anticipated when the circuits generating these signals were designed. This delay can be reduced in several ways. The on-chip InCheck generation circuit can be made much faster along with the output pads that drive the wired-OR status lines. Two different pads should be used for the two different check signals. Although they cannot be generated at the same time, they can be latched and the time required to drive the signals off-chip overlapped with other functions. Since these signals are rarely asserted, they can be checked by a later microinstruction. These changes would reduce the total search time by at least 4.0%.

Latch Next Move This operation only latches the result of the move generation circuit and priority PLA into a voter register and as such should be quite fast. The length of this operation is caused by a design flaw in the testing/debugging shift register that introduced a substantial load on one of the bits in the voter register. Fixing this simple design error would speed the search by 3.8%.

Push Move/Pop Move These stack operations incur no overhead at all. Although their execution can be overlapped with the execution of a halfmove, this is unnecessary since a free cycle is available for the move generator in the microprogram.

6.3.2 Hash Table Delay

Reading an entry from the hash table requires 300 ns. or 5 subcycles. The hash table read that is done for every position is done in parallel with other operations, since the result is not used immediately. Writing the hash table first requires a read cycle to determine whether the entry can be written and then a write cycle. This takes 13 subcycles, ignoring the privilege depth calculation, during which no other function is performed. But since an entry is written relatively infrequently, reducing the time to write an entry into the hash table to zero would reduce the total search time by only 2.8%.

6.3.3 Evaluation Delay

Updating the evaluation state variables with each halfmove is done very quickly since it involves only clocking new values into the evaluation input registers. The delay from the time the state registers are changed until the evaluation function value is valid may be quite long, involving the delay through at least one level of alterable PLA and through the adder tree. From the flow graph, it can be seen that there are several cycles from the time the last halfmove is executed until the evaluation value is used. Currently this time is 810 ns., but if the time required by the move generator were reduced as described above, this time would become only 510 ns. In Hitech, which only simulates the VLSI evaluation design, the evaluation delay is about 350 ns. Designing a VLSI chip for general evaluation that meets these timing requirements would not be difficult.

6.4 Analysis of the Move Generator Move Ordering

One of the advantages of the move generator architecture is the ability to order moves using information similar to that gained by a two ply search. All moves are evaluated according to any capture and possible recapture. In this section, we measure the search efficiency attained by this move ordering and compare it to the optimal ordering and the ordering produced by alternative move generator designs. Since the hash table affects the move ordering by providing the best move found by the previous iteration, we begin by analyzing this effect of the hash table on move ordering. We also measure the effect of the hash table size.

Most of the results in this section are presented by comparing the size of search trees resulting from different search methods. For example, the efficiencies attained by various move orderings are compared by examining the ratio of their search sizes. We will see that our move generator ordering results in searches that are only about 1.4 times as large as the smallest possible α-β search. Most of the results in this section were obtained by running Hitech on a set of ten positions comprising five tactical and five positional problems. These positions all examine between 100,000 and 300,000 positions over a six ply search. The tactical problems involve tactics that occur at five and six ply. The results for tactical problems are shown in the graphs as dashed lines while positional problems are shown as dotted lines. Since the different move orderings were simulated in software, deeper searches were not practical. Tests which do not have these restrictions use a larger set of general problems.

6.4.1 The Effect of the Hash Table on Search Efficiency

The move ordering is greatly affected by the use of the hash table to save the best move discovered by earlier search iterations. This effect is summarized in Figure 6.9, which compares Hitech's performance when using moves from the hash table to its performance when not using this source of information. These results are given as a ratio in search sizes between the two cases. This experiment shows that the size of the search when not using moves from the hash table is about twice as large as when using the moves. Moreover, the ratio becomes greater as the search depth is increased, since the move ordering near the root of the tree has more effect. Since searches to depth eight and greater are most important, we conclude that not using the hash table for moves affects the search size by at least a factor of two. One way to make up for not using the hash table to save moves from one iteration to the next is to save the first few ply of the tree in main memory[9].

This graph also indicates a relationship between the search depth and the relative efficiency achieved by using the hash table to improve move ordering. This improvement is greater at even plies than at odd plies. When a four ply search is performed, the search is generating the moves for almost all the nodes at depth three for the first time. Since these are β nodes, the number of moves generated before a refutation is found depends on how well the moves are ordered. When searching to five ply, the nodes being expanded at the frontier are α_2 nodes, where the move ordering is irrelevant. This effect can be seen in the results throughout this section: a better move ordering has more effect at the even search depths. This would be even more noticeable if the search did not extend lines that involve checks, which cause less uniform

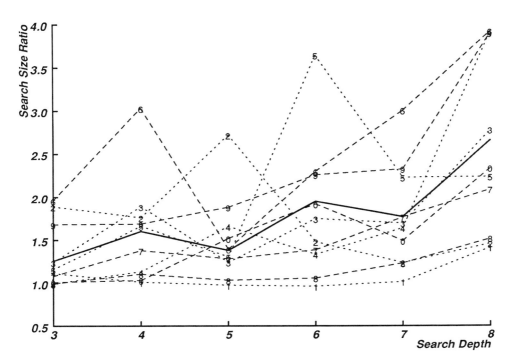

Figure 6.9: *The effect of not saving moves in the hash table is to increase the search size by a factor of two. The FIFO replacement algorithm was used when detecting transpositions only, since that produces the best performance. The hash table size is 1024K entries.*

trees.

We should also note that the results of this experiment depend on the move generator ordering. A poorer move ordering than that produced by the Hitech move generator would result in an even greater disparity in search sizes.

The graph in Figure 6.10 shows the effect of the size of the hash table on the search performance. In this experiment, the privilege depth value was adjusted according to the size of the hash table to produce the best performance for each table size. The slope of the lines from 16K to 1024K entries over all sizes of search is about $-.07$, meaning that each doubling in the hash table size yields only a 7% decrease in the search size. If this effect

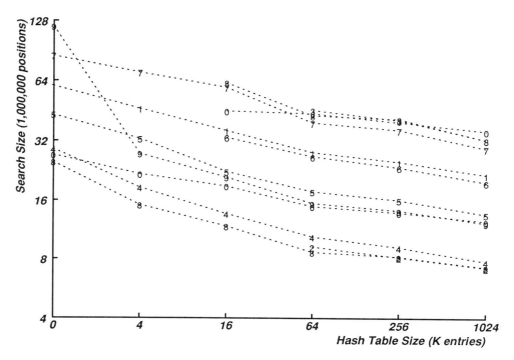

Figure 6.10: *The effect of hash table size on search efficiency.*

can be extrapolated, and there are indications that the slope is decreasing, then an 8 million entry table would perform only about 20% better than the current hash table. In fact, the hash table used originally had 256K entries and was only about 15% less effective than the current 1024K entry table.

The effectiveness of dividing the nodes in the tree into privileged nodes, which are replaced in the hash table only by deeper results, and non-privileged nodes, which are replaced in simple FIFO order, can be seen in Figure 6.11. These measurements were done using a 16K entry hash table so that the effect of splitting the hash table is clear. This experiment performed eight ply searches on several different problems, each represented by one line in this graph, varying the privilege depth of the hash table from three to eight. The results presented compare the size of each of these searches to the search size when the hash table is not split. Since these are eight ply searches, setting the privilege depth to eight is equivalent to not splitting

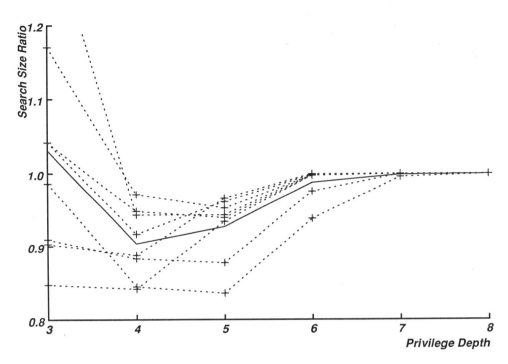

Figure 6.11: *The effect of using a hybrid replacement scheme for the hash table. The results are given here for eight ply searches and a 16K entry hash table.*

the hash table at all. For this size table, a privilege depth of four results in a search size about 5 to 15% smaller than if the hash table is not split. For normal searches of depth eight or nine using the 1024K entry table, splitting the hash table produces a speedup of only about 5%. However, for deeper searches found in the endgame, this optimization often produces as much as a factor of two speedup, since the number of possible transpositions within a single subtree is greatly increased.

Setting the privilege depth to four means that most of the tree down to depth four is locked in the hash table. For these searches, this corresponds to about 20,000 nodes or about 15% of the hash table. This appears to be about the best figure for a range of hash table sizes. Hitech uses a privilege depth of seven for its 1024K entry hash table.

The FIFO replacement algorithm corresponds to setting the privilege depth to zero. This graph indicates that the search size increases if the privilege depth is set too low, implying that FIFO is not effective when using the hash table for both move ordering and detecting transpositions.

6.4.2   The Move Generator Move Ordering

The best possible move ordering is achieved if the first move tried at α nodes always results in the best value and if the first move tried at β nodes always provides a refutation. Both the move generator and the hash table contribute to the actual move ordering used by the search. If the values assigned to the nodes of a search tree do not change much from one iteration to the next, the move stored in the hash table is very likely to be the right move to try first in the next search iteration. In this case, if the hash table is large enough to contain the whole tree, the move ordering at all the internal nodes of the tree is determined wholly by the hash table, and the move generator move ordering is important only at the leaf nodes, which were not reached by the previous search iteration.

We have measured the efficiency of the search conducted by Hitech by comparing the number of positions it searches to the number of positions it would search if the move ordering it used were perfect. This perfect ordering was approximated by performing a search and storing the best move for each position in the hash table. The *values* in the hash table were then invalidated and the search performed again. Since the move ordering is entirely determined by the hash table, which has the best move for every position, the search should examine the minimum number of positions allowed by the α-β algorithm. This move ordering is only approximately optimal because not all the positions can be stored in the hash table. Since the hash table has one million entries, the size of the searches used to measure the optimal move ordering was restricted to about 200,000 positions, corresponding to seven ply searches. These search trees are almost completely stored in the hash table, and those positions not in the hash table are almost always near the leaves where their effect on the overall result is minimal.

The results of comparing the move generator ordering to the optimal move ordering are presented in Figure 6.12. These results compare the search size achieved by Hitech's move generator ordering to that possible with a perfect ordering. This ratio is less than 1.5, meaning that the Hitech move ordering achieves a search efficiency that is within 50% of optimal.

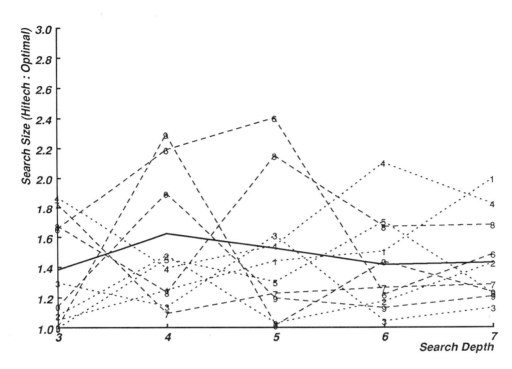

Figure 6.12: *A comparison of search tree sizes resulting from the move generator ordering to those achieved by optimal move ordering. The hash table size is 1024K entries.*

We also compared the move ordering of the move generator to that of other move generators that have been used. Simulating other move orderings introduced substantial overhead into the search, allowing searches of only depth six to be used for gathering statistics. Since the large hash table has a much greater effect on the move ordering for these small searches, the hash table size was reduced to 16K entries when performing these move ordering comparisons. This gives about the same 25:1 ratio between the tree size and hash table size that the search normally encounters in a three minute search. The following move ordering experiments all use the hash table to improve the move ordering.

An example of a move ordering used by many programs is the use of the evaluation function to order the moves based on the positions reached

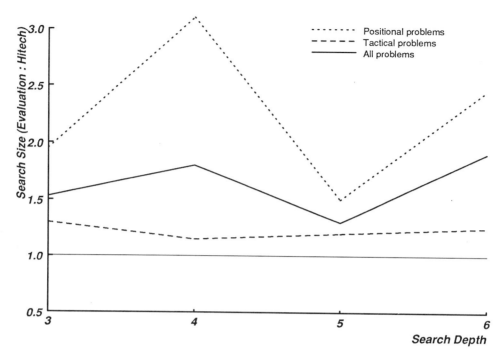

Figure 6.13: *A comparison of evaluation move ordering with the Hitech move generator ordering.*

by each move. This requires generating all moves, evaluating the position reached by each, and sorting the moves based on this value. The comparison between this ordering by evaluation function and Hitech's ordering is shown in Figure 6.13. The search sizes resulting from the evaluation ordering are an average of about 1.5 times that resulting from the move generator ordering.

A second move ordering that we measured is that of Belle's move generator. Recall that Belle's move ordering produces the most valuable captures first and non-captures last, with ties broken by moving the least valuable pieces first. The comparison between Belle's move ordering and Hitech's move ordering is given in Figure 6.14. Hitech's move ordering also produces a speedup of about 1.5 over Belle's move ordering. In fact, by basing the ordering on the material gained by each move, Belle is approximating a one ply evaluation-based ordering using only material. Belle's ordering

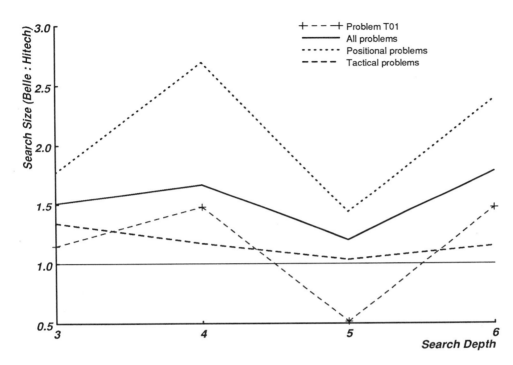

Figure 6.14: *A comparison between Hitech's and Belle's move ordering.*

uses somewhat more information by taking into account the value of the capturing piece, but using the evaluation function allows positional factors to order moves that don't involve material exchange. We should note that the move ordering measured here includes using the hash table to affect the move ordering, whereas Belle does not store moves in the hash table.

Hitech's improved ordering appears to make a much greater difference for positional problems than it does for tactical problems. We conjecture that this is so because there are more reasonable moves in quiet positions, and the subtrees searched after these reasonable moves provide fewer easy choices for the move ordering. In other words, simple captures are more likely to produce a refutation in tactical positions than in quiet positions. Since positions that are encountered in games are more likely to be quiet than tactical, the better move ordering produced by Hitech may have more of an overall effect than indicated here.

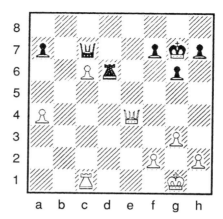

Figure 6.15: *Black to move. In this position Hitech's move ordering performs worse than simpler orderings based on a one ply search.*

These results do not mean that Hitech's move ordering is always better. Consider the position in Figure 6.15 which is the position T01 referred to in the graph in Figure 6.14. At ply five, Hitech's move ordering results in a search that is about 50% larger than either of the simpler orderings. What happens is that the search discovers for the first time during the five ply search that the queen sacrifice, Qe5, f6, QxR, QxQ, wins because it can be followed by c7. Any move ordering based on a one ply search rates QxR best since it gains the most material. Hitech, correctly judging that QxR loses material since it is followed by QxQ, produces this move much later in the move ordering. In this case, the sacrifice happens to be the right move; however, most of the time Hitech's move ordering would be vindicated.

6.4.3   Host Software and Move Ordering

We have mentioned that the move ordering can be improved by storing part of the search tree near the root in main memory. Although this is not so important if moves are stored in the hash table, even then it can sometimes have a large effect on the time of the search. Hitech only stores the first ply of the tree in main memory, and in some positions this can cause the search tree to be much larger than necessary.

Consider the search tree of Figure 6.16 where the value of the first move

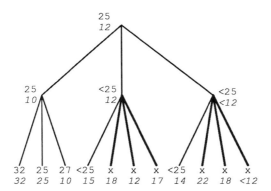

Figure 6.16: *If the value of the search changes drastically from one iteration to the next, the search must examine subtrees not encountered during previous iterations. These new subtrees are indicated by the bold lines. The values returned by the depth eight search are shown first followed in italics by the values returned by the depth nine search.*

has been found to be 25 by a depth eight search and the second and third moves have been refuted by finding an opponent move with a value of less than 25. Now at depth nine suppose that the value of the first move is found to be only 10. If the refutation move found by the eight ply search happens to have a value less than 10, then it is still valid and the tree does not change. If, however, the value of this move is more than 10, as shown in this example, then the search must examine more moves to find a refutation, or all the moves if there is no refutation and it is the case that the second move is better than the first. In either case, the search must perform depth eight subsearches on positions that have not been seen in previous searches. Since no suggested move is to be found in the hash table, these searches may be very inefficient unless the move generator move ordering is very good.

This problem became apparent as a result of a weakness in the move generator ordering. Pawn advances to the last rank are not treated differently from other pawn advances, even though they imply a large change in material and should be examined first—even before queen captures. In the position shown in Figure 6.17, this problem occurs during a depth eight search when considering the line Re8, Kg7. Although the best refutation is clearly h8=Q,

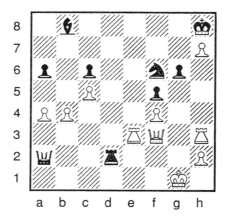

Figure 6.17: *White to move.*

the move generator produces QxP as the first move, which is a sufficient refutation until the search reaches eight ply. Since the pawn promotion move occurs almost at the end of the move ordering, the search must then perform many six ply searches before finding the 'obvious' refutation. To make matters worse, these lines include many checks that extend the searches even further. While the seven ply search takes only eight seconds, the eight ply search requires 20 minutes.

Iterative deepening is meant to solve exactly this problem. By saving the best moves found by previous searches, the move ordering in subsequent searches can be made near-optimal. If the search must examine new ground, this source of move ordering information is unavailable. The solution then is to apply iterative deepening recursively at those positions for which the search has no previous information and where the consequences may be great. While the search consistently breaks new ground near the leaves of the tree, the consequences are minimal; but if this happens near the root on a deep search, then the penalty can be substantial. The microcode was modified to test whether these situations could be identified and corrected. The microcode looked for positions near the root for which the refutation move in the hash table was unlikely to be sufficient, and recursively applied iterative deepening from these positions. For the position of Figure 6.17, this reduced the time for an eight ply search from 20 minutes to 20 seconds. Although this search optimization can be performed in microcode, recognizing all the cases for which this should be done is complicated and is more suited to the host program. Fortunately for Hitech, the move ordering provided by the move generator is good enough that this problem does not occur very often. In the case of pawn promotion, special hardware was added to recognize imminent pawn promotions and treat them specially.

6.5   Redesigning the Move Generator

The measurements presented in Figure 6.4, 6.5, and 6.6 show that it is the move generator that constrains the speed of the search. Some of the move generator operations have satisfactory performance in the current implementation, in particular the execution of halfmoves and the stack operations, but other operations cause performance bottlenecks. The problems with the operations that generate the check status signals and latch the next move are easily rectified as discussed in Sections 6.3.1 and 6.3.1 by fixing oversights in the current implementation. Other problems are not so easily remedied.

Voting is a fundamental bottleneck in the current implementation because of the inherent delay in the distributed voting algorithm and the number of voting cycles that must be performed. We have discussed how the voting delay is currently reduced by using external buffers to drive the vote bus. The delay can also be reduced by improving the drive capability of the output pads. Is there some way to reduce or eliminate the number of voting cycles that are required to generate the best move?

Two of the four cycles in the voting sequence described in Section 3.2.5 are used to discriminate between moves on the basis of a dynamic priority calculation, and the remaining two are used only to identify one move when more than one has the same priority. A much faster way to perform this second operation is with an ordinary priority encoder tree arranged to produce moves to the center first. Although this enforces a static centrality measure, the value of being able to change the centrality metric has not been established and is probably minimal. We cannot use the same technique to avoid the first two vote cycles without losing all ordering information, but we can reduce these two cycles to one by reducing the granularity of the dynamic priority value. We propose then to replace the current voting implementation by one which performs one vote based on a 4-bit priority to determine those chips with a highest priority move. The chips identified by this cycle would assert a signal that is input to an external priority circuit that selects

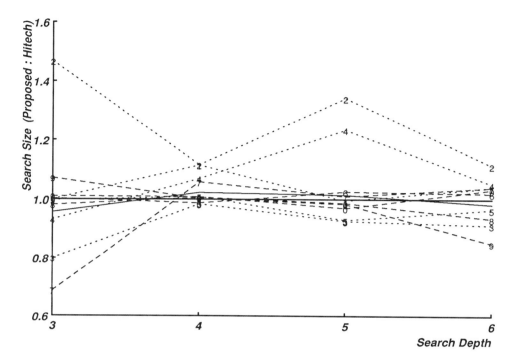

Figure 6.18: *A comparison of the proposed voting procedure with the current implementation. The change in the search efficiency is negligible.*

the most central chip. The time required for the voting cycle would be reduced because the vote bus could be precharged well in advance of the vote. Thus the delay for the entire voting procedure would be determined by the time to drive the vote bus, the time to assert a priority output and the delay through the priority encoder tree.

Measurements were performed to determine the effect of reducing the range of the dynamic priority value, and the results are shown in Figure 6.18. These measurements also assume that the pawn advance moves are placed in the correct order instead of after queen moves as in the current implementation. In fact neither of these changes affects the move ordering very much. The proposed voting scheme reduces the time spent voting from the current 19.2% to less than 6% with no loss in search efficiency.

The improved move ordering achieved by this design does cost a certain amount in terms of chip area. A number of tradeoffs are possible if we wish to reduce the chip size. As Hsu[15] has noted, if all the moves are generated for one destination square before generating the moves for another destination square, there is no need for the on-chip context stack. Instead, an external stack saves the chip number and move index of the previous move generated. When called upon to generate the next move, the chip is again accessed, given the previous move index and asked to output the next move. If there are no moves to that square, some mechanism is invoked to determine the next destination square. There must also be some way to keep previous squares with the same priority from voting. In our case, the priority value last generated would be broadcast first to keep previous chips from voting. This change in the move extraction procedure does not greatly change the move ordering. For α_2 nodes, where all moves must be generated, the move ordering has no effect anyway. For β and α_1 nodes, the first move generated is the same as before. Only in those cases where this move is not best will the different move ordering have an effect.

The size of the PLA that computes the dynamic priority value can also be reduced by simplifying the criteria used to select the best move. The pawn guard information is much more important in the current implementation than the piece guard information. Using only the capture information and the pawn guards to compute priority would reduce the size of the PLA by a factor of four.

The result of making these changes to the move generator is a much smaller chip since the context stack is eliminated and the size of the priority PLA reduced. The move ordering would result in search sizes somewhere between that achieved by Hitech and Belle's move ordering, an increase of as much as 50%. The benefits to be gained from a smaller chip implementation must be weighed against the decrease in performance. If the smaller chip results in a smaller number of chips and faster operation, overall performance may not be affected very much.

The size of the chip can also be reduced by other means, for example, by eliminating some of the debugging circuitry used in the current implementation and by better floorplanning. Combined, these changes would allow the square size to be halved. Another implementation option is wafer-scale integration. Since the connections between chips are bussed, simple wiring in the channels is sufficient for wiring the array. By providing a number of redundant squares on the wafer, yield problems can be overcome. The selection method would have to be different if redundant squares are used since the layout of working cells cannot be assumed to be a simple 8 by 8 array. Instead of the standard 2D select circuit, the selection would have to be done by broadcasting the actual address of the square to be selected. Since most operations are done with all chips selected, and those that aren't do not use the input bus, this does not require any extra wires.

Wafer scale integration is also appropriate for the evaluation chip. The input bus and control are broadcast to all chips. The outputs are simply fed into an adder tree, which can be implemented within the cells using the standard H-tree layout.

6.6   Conclusions

This chapter has presented evidence of the effectiveness of the distributed state architecture for move generation and position evaluation. Hitech's speed and knowledge are the result of full-scale implementations of this architecture for these two problems. While these are prototypes and, as such, can be improved, Hitech's success has already proved that this architecture is an effective solution in the domain of chess.

The measurements of the Hitech hardware have shown that the supporting hardware and software system has not hidden the performance of the move generator and evaluation function. The speed of the rest of the hardware has allowed us to measure the real performance of the move generator. Our measurements have also shown how important it is to use the hash table to improve move ordering. Even for Hitech's improved move ordering, this can reduce the search size by a factor of two. The move generator's ability to answer queries about the legality of moves stored in the hash table allows us to use this information without risk. These measurements also show that the effort devoted to move ordering in the move generator pays off by reducing the search size by a factor of 1.5 over simpler move orderings. Moreover, there is evidence that the move ordering is even more important as one searches deeper.

Although we have found several ways to improve the performance of the current implementation, the prototype has proved the effectiveness of this VLSI architecture for move generation. In comparison to other hardware move generators that use what are effectively carry chains to simulate moves, move generation is essentially instantaneous in this architecture compared to the problems of getting information on and off the chips. We see no difficulty in taking advantage of the ever-increasing levels of integration provided by advancing technology. We estimate that a combination of the improvements suggested in the chapter, more aggressive circuit design, and current CMOS technology would result in an implementation with at least five times the performance of the current one.

7

Conclusion

This thesis has presented a VLSI architecture for move generation and position evaluation for chess along with results based on a full-scale implementation of this architecture. The resulting chess system, Hitech, has surpassed all previous efforts in computer chess by 150 rating points. Moreover, all indications are that Hitech will continue to improve in the near future. Improvement will be possible because this architecture allows the chess knowledge used for position evaluation to be extended almost indefinitely without significantly affecting the speed of the search.

A key feature of this architecture is the idea of *distributed state*. Both the move generator and position evaluator consist of many independent functional units, each of which maintains the state that is relevant to the function that unit computes. This state is updated as the search is performed by broadcasting *changes* in the system state to all functional units. In chess, where the difference between adjacent positions in the search tree can be encoded very succinctly, the overhead required to keep the distributed state up to date is small, allowing the search tree to be traversed very quickly. By computing the many individual functions required by move generation and position evaluation in parallel, this architecture reduces the time spent on these complex components to close to that spent on the search control itself. Moreover, because of the limited communication and the regularity of the architecture, its size and performance scale well with advances in technology.

7.1 Move Generation

The speed of the α-β search is bounded by the move generator, both in terms of its speed and the search efficiency that results from the order in which moves are produced. The move generator we have designed and implemented using this architecture operates at up to 200,000 moves per second with a move ordering that results in search trees less than 1.5 times larger than the smallest possible with α-β search. This compares to a figure of about 2.2 attained by Belle's move ordering. The move ordering is done using information about the moves available to both players to estimate the outcome of each move with approximately the same accuracy as a two ply search. We have reached the point where further effort spent on move ordering will not produce large gains in search efficiency.

The measurements of the move generator performance presented in Chapter 6 suggest a number of changes to the move generator. The major improvement involves the voting procedure that determines the destination square of the best move. By reducing the range of values used for the dynamic priority assigned to moves and using an external priority encoder, the time spent on this operation can be reduced from an average of three cycles to a single cycle. Moreover, this cycle can be shortened since the time required to charge the voting bus can be overlapped with other operations. The performance of this move generator also scales well with advances in technology so that a move generator built with current technology and incorporating the changes that we have suggested would be able to produce moves at a rate in excess of 1,000,000 per second and would require only eight chips.

7.2 Position Evaluation

The chess-playing ability of a program is determined by a combination of the search depth and the amount of evaluation performed on each position examined by the search. This has led to the problem of deciding how much chess knowledge to incorporate in light of its effect on the search speed. The architecture described in this thesis for position evaluation effectively solves this problem by allowing complex evaluation to be performed extremely quickly. This is done by breaking the evaluation into a number of independent components, each of which can be computed in parallel over some subset of the board state. The results are then added in $O(log)$ time using an adder tree.

In Chapter 4 we described the complexity of evaluation components in terms of first and second-order evaluations and described a VLSI chip for computing second-order evaluation. We then described how several of the more common evaluation components can be computed using this chip.

While we have not implemented this chip, the position evaluation performed by Hitech simulates this architecture using standard circuit components. The quality of Hitech's play shows that this is indeed an extremely effective evaluation method. We estimate the value of the second-order evaluation of Hitech to be 150 rating points for the pawn structure evaluation alone and 200 rating points for the remaining second-order evaluation components.

The usefulness of this evaluation hardware derives from more than just its computational power. First, the actual functions that the hardware performs are programmable. This means that the chess knowledge included in the evaluation can be changed and refined as we discover the effect of different kinds of knowledge. It also allows the host program to modify the evaluation function to suit the region of the search over the course of a game. Even more important is the ability to increase the amount of chess knowledge by simply adding more evaluation hardware. Doubling the number of components evaluated adds only constant time, that of a single addition, to the evaluation time. We cannot predict how far this evaluation method will take us, but for the foreseeable future, progress will be limited more by what we know about chess knowledge rather than by any limits imposed by the hardware.

7.3   Contributions

The contributions of this thesis are a *VLSI architecture* for chess move generation and evaluation, an *implementation* of a full-scale chess machine using this architecture, and a *performance analysis* of this hardware.

1. *A VLSI architecture that is effective for chess move generation and evaluation.* The bulk of this thesis has been concerned with the description of hardware implementations of these two operations. The success of Hitech has demonstrated that this architecture is indeed a good solution for chess. Moreover, the nature of the architecture allows further performance improvements to be accomplished by taking advantage of future technological developments and by increasing the amount of chess knowledge applied to position evaluation.

2. *The implementation of a full-scale chess machine.* This machine provides a vehicle for further research into the problem of computer chess. We see this research following two paths. The first is the extension of the

position evaluation used by Hitech. This requires a better understanding of the knowledge required to make a brute-force search capable of playing top-flight chess, and perhaps additional hardware as the amount and types of knowledge required exceeds the capability of the current implementation. The second path involves experiments with different search algorithms. The Hitech hardware is sufficiently flexible that experiments using different types of search are possible. The performance of the hardware will make the results of these experiments meaningful.

3. *An analysis of the performance of this hardware implementation.* We have presented detailed measurements of the performance of the move generator in the context of Hitech. These measurements support our conclusion about the effectiveness of the architecture and point to those parts of the implementation that can be improved. These measurements also show that the move ordering performed by the move generator is very close to optimal. Measurements on the effect of the hash table show that using the hash table to improve move ordering speeds the search by at least a factor of two, and that doubling the size of the hash table over a range of sizes speeds the search by only 7%.

7.4   Future Work

Future work on the ideas of this thesis falls into two categories: a continuation of the work in the domain of chess, and the investigation of the applicability of this architecture to other problems.

7.4.1   Chess

One of the contributions of this thesis is a chess machine that can be used to investigate some of the important questions facing computer chess. The flexibility of the control structure allows experiments with different search algorithms. There have been efforts at defining selective search algorithms that reduce the size of the search. In our case, selective search would be useful to search more deeply in those situations that involve deep tactical ideas. While forward pruning is very dangerous, it has been suggested that the search should identify those lines of play that must be searched more deeply because they contain tactics that must be understood. This approach trades one or two plies of search for an extension along a few important lines.

How these lines of play are identified is the subject of continuing research. The raw speed of the hardware also makes possible experiments with parallel search algorithms that have been suggested for both small and large numbers of processors.

We see the most important future work with Hitech to be done in the area of position evaluation. This work is already under way by Hans Berliner with excellent prospects for better understanding of what kinds of chess knowledge lead to world-championship play. The relationship between knowledge and deep search is also a subject for further research, as it is still not well understood how deep search affects the type of knowledge that is required to produce a desired behavior. We saw a hint of this in Chapter 4 where a deeper search allowed knowledge of pins to be omitted from position evaluation. We expect a better understanding of this phenomenon to be important to other problems in Artificial Intelligence.

We have identified some ways to improve the implementation of the move generator chip and indicated how improved technology can be used to make a smaller and faster move generator. We believe that for the immediate future the primary route to improved chess-playing performance is through improved chess knowledge in the evaluation function. The current search speed of Hitech is certainly sufficient for this investigation. Indeed, Hitech already outperforms other computer programs. It is best to wait until we have a better understanding of the effect of speed and knowledge on performance before building new hardware. It may be that another order of magnitude of speed is required to produce world-class chess in this type of brute-force program. If so, experience over the next two or three years should reveal this, and by that time the technology to achieve this performance gain will be available.

7.4.2   Other Applications

We expect the distributed state architecture used in Hitech to be effective in domains other than chess. While previous solutions to move generation and position evaluation have been tailored to chess, it is clear that our solution would remain valid even if the rules of chess were changed drastically. It is easy to see how this architecture can be used for other games such as checkers and Othello, although it is less obvious to see how well it would apply to Go. We believe that research should be conducted to determine the generality of this architecture and its effectiveness with respect to other problems.

This research should attempt to characterize the properties of problems that can be solved effectively by this architecture. We conjecture that the following types of problems can benefit from this approach.

- Search problems. Search often requires decisions to be made at every point in the search space, and this means that other forms of parallelism such as pipelining and multiprocessor systems are less than effective solutions. We have described an architecture in this thesis that applies fine-grained parallelism to the computation required at each node, allowing the search to proceed rapidly through the search space.

- Problems with well-defined state information. This architecture operates over subsets of the system state that are defined ahead of time. If one does not know what states the system can reach, then one cannot define the functions over that state.

- Problems for which the transitions from one state to the next can be encoded succinctly. Although one can imagine the distributed state being entirely rewritten for every state change, this cost would completely dominate the time taken for the computation over the resulting state. Problems in which the state changes incrementally from one point to the next can take advantage of the fast computation afforded by this architecture.

- Evaluation problems that can be divided into individual components that can be solved independently.

We believe that some good candidate problems are those that involve low-level perception; some problems in speech recognition and low-level vision present possibilities. Other problems that have been suggested are the analysis and synthesis of molecular structures and automatic programming.

Researchers in computer chess have long been faced with a tradeoff between search speed and chess knowledge. The architecture described in this thesis solves this problem for chess, permitting a large advance in the state of the art of computer chess. We have not yet reached the limit of this solution; it will be some time before we understand how far this architecture will carry us towards championship level chess.

Bibliography

[1] O. Babaoglu. *A Hardware Move Generator for Chess*. Tech Report, University of California, Berkeley, 1977.

[2] H. J. Berliner. Personal Communication, 1985.

[3] H. J. Berliner. The B* tree search algorithm: A best-first proof procedure. *Artificial Intelligence*, 12(1):23–40, 1979.

[4] H. J. Berliner. *Chess as Problem Solving: The Developments of a Tactics Analyzer*. PhD thesis, Carnegie-Mellon University, July 1974.

[5] H. J. Berliner. An examination of brute force intelligence. In *Proceedings of the 7th International Joint Conference on Artificial Intelligence*, pages 581–587, IJCAI, 1981.

[6] H. J. Berliner. On the construction of evaluation functions for large domains. In *Sixth International Joint Conference on Artificial Intelligence*, pages 53–55, IJCAI, August 1979.

[7] H. J. Berliner and C. Ebeling. The SUPREM architecture: A new intelligent paradigm. *Artificial Intelligence*, 28(1):3–8, February 1986.

[8] M. Campbell and H. J. Berliner. Personal communication, 1986.

[9] J. H. Condon and K. Thompson. Belle chess hardware. In *Advances in Computer Chess III*, Pergamon Press, 1982.

[10] R. A. Finkel and J. P. Fishburn. Parallelism in alpha-beta search. *Artificial Intelligence*, 19:89–106, 1982.

[11] P. W. Frey. An introduction to computer chess. In P. W. Frey, editor, *Chess Skill in Man and Machine*, chapter 3, pages 54–81, Springer-Verlag, 1983.

[12] J. J. Gillogly. *Performance Analysis of the Technology Chess Program*. PhD thesis, Carnegie-Mellon University, 1978.

[13] J. J. Gillogly. The Technology chess program. *Artificial Intelligence*, 3:145–163, 1972.

[14] G. Goetsch. Personal Communication, 1986.

[15] F. Hsu. *Two Designs of Functional Units for VLSI Based Chess Machines*. Tech Report CMU-CS-86-103, Carnegie-Mellon University, January 1986.

[16] D. E. Knuth and R. W. Moore. An analysis of alpha-beta pruning. *Artificial Intelligence*, 6:293–326, 1975.

[17] J. F. P. Marchand. An alterable programmable logic array. *IEEE Journal of Solid-State Physics*, SC-20(5):1061–1066, October 1985.

[18] T. A. Marsland, M. Olafsson, and J. Schaeffer. Multiprocessor tree-search experiments. In *Advances in Computer Chess 4*, pages 37–51, Pergamon Press, 1985.

[19] J. Moussouris, J. Holloway, and R. Greenblatt. CHEOPS: A chess-oriented processing system. In D. Michie, J.E. Hayes and L.I. Mikulich, editors, *Machine Intelligence 9*, Wiley & Sons, Chichester, Sussex, England, 1979.

[20] H. L. Nelson. Hash tables in Cray Blitz. *ICCA Journal*, 3–13, March 1985.

[21] A. Newell, J. Shaw, and H. Simon. Chess playing programs and the problem of complexity. *IBM Journal of Research and Development*, 2:320–335, 1958.

[22] A. J. Palay. *Searching with Probabilities*. PhD thesis, Carnegie-Mellon University, May 1983.

[23] R. D. Greenblatt et. al. The Greenblatt chess program. In *Proceedings of the Fall Joint Computer Conference*, pages 801–810, ACM, 1967.

[24] A. L. Samuel. Some studies in machine learning using the game of checkers, recent progress. *IBM Journal of Research and Development*, 601–617, November 1967.

[25] J. Schaeffer, P. Powell, and J. Jonkman. A VLSI chess legal move generator. In R. Bryant, editor, *Proceedings of the Third Caltech Conference on Very Large Scale Integration*, California Institute of Technology, March 1983.

[26] C. E. Shannon. Programming a computer for playing chess. *Philosophical Magazine*, 41(314):256–275, 1950.

[27] J. R. Slagle and J. K. Dixon. Experiments with some programs that search game trees. *Journal of the ACM*, 16(2):189–207, 1969.

[28] D. J. Slate and L. R. Atkin. Chess 4.5 - The Northwestern University chess program. In P. W. Frey, editor, *Chess Skill in Man and Machine*, Springer-Verlag, Berlin, 1977.

[29] K. Thompson. Personal Communication, 1984.

[30] K. Thompson. Computer chess strength. In *Advances in Computer Chess III*, pages 55–56, Pergamon Press, 1982.

[31] A. L. Zobrist. *A Hashing Method with Applications for Game Playing*. Tech Report 88, Computer Science Department, University of Wisconsin, 1970.

Index

The MIT Press, with Peter Denning, general consulting editor, and Brian Randell, European consulting editor, publishes computer science books in the following series:

ACM Doctoral Dissertation Award and Distinguished Dissertation Series

Artificial Intelligence, Patrick Winston and Michael Brady, editors

Charles Babbage Institute Reprint Series for the History of Computing, Martin Campbell-Kelly, editor

Computer Systems, Herb Schwetman, editor

Explorations in Logo, E. Paul Goldenberg, editor

Foundations of Computing, Michael Garey, editor

History of Computing, I. Bernard Cohen and William Aspray, editors

Information Systems, Michael Lesk, editor

Logic Programming, Ehud Shapiro, editor; Fernando Pereira, Koichi Furukawa, and D. H. D. Warren, associate editors

The MIT Electrical Engineering and Computer Science Series

Scientific Computation, Dennis Gannon, editor